Lanz
Fuerteventura

Text by Pam Barrett
Edited by Alex Knights
Principal photographer: Neil Buchan-Grant
Series Editor: Tony Halliday

Berlitz POCKET GUIDE

Lanzarote & Fuerteventura

First Edition 2007

NO part of this book may be reproduced, stored in a retrieval system or transmitted in any form or means electronic, mechanical, photocopying, recording or otherwise, without prior written permission from Berlitz Publishing. Brief text quotations with use of photographs are exempted for book review purposes only.

PHOTOGRAPHY

All photography by Neil Buchan-Grant/APA except: Andrew Eames 15; Fonnollosa/Prisma Archivo Fotografico 18; Eric Roberts 33; Glyn Genin 97; Profimedia International s.r.o./Alamy 99; Chris Coe 100
Cover photograph: J. Miller/Robert Harding Picture Library/Alamy

CONTACTING THE EDITORS

Every effort has been made to provide accurate information in this publication, but changes are inevitable. The publisher cannot be responsible for any resulting loss, inconvenience or injury. We would appreciate it if readers would call our attention to any errors or outdated information by contacting Berlitz Publishing, PO Box 7910, London SE1 1WE, England.
Fax: (44) 20 7403 0290
Email: berlitz@apaguide.co.uk
<www.berlitzpublishing.com>

The islands' windmills are a reminder of a time before tourism

Great sweeps of white sand draw the visitors to Fuerteventura's Costa Calma beaches (page 75)

Timanfaya (page 52) has unforgettable volcanic landscape

TOP TEN ATTRACTIONS

A sandstone doorway adorns the church in the pretty village of Pájara (page 73) ▼

◄ Former capital of Lanzarote, Teguise (page 44) is an attractive town that holds a busy market every Sunday

Lanzarote's biggest resort, Puerto del Carmen (page 49) offers some of the island's best beaches ►

The Fundación César Manrique (page 41) was the home of Lanzarote's iconic artist and architect ▼

➤ A cool trip, the dramatic lava-formed Cueva de los Verdes (page 34)

Cobbled streets and courtyards, 15th-century Betancuria (page 70) ➤

Outside cheerful Corralejo town lie the great empty swathes of Fuerteventura's El Jable dunes (page 67) ➤

CONTENTS

A ➤ in the text denotes a highly recommended sight

Fact Sheets

INTRODUCTION

Swept by trade winds and warmed by coastal currents, the islands of Lanzarote and Fuerteventura offer a consistently warm climate, with some 300 days of sunshine a year. They are part of the Canary Islands, which lie approximately 1,100km (690 miles) southwest of the Spanish mainland and, at the nearest point, 115km (70 miles) from the West African coast. The islands are part of Spain, but since 1982 have formed an autonomous province, divided in two: the eastern islands, which include Lanzarote and Fuerteventura, are governed by a Cabildo Insular (Island Council) from Las Palmas de Gran Canaria, the western islands from Santa Cruz de Tenerife.

Lanzarote is some 60km (38 miles) in length and 24km (15 miles) across at its widest point, with a population of about 116,000, of whom some 48,000 live in the capital, Arrecife. Fuerteventura is larger, at around 100km (60 miles) long and 30km (18 miles) wide, but sparsely populated – there are around 79,000 inhabitants, of whom about half live in Puerto del Rosario.

Landscape and Climate

The whole volcanic archipelago is barren, but Lanzarote and Fuerteventura are drier and more barren than the rest. Lanzarote's last volcanic explosion was in 1824, but the heat is still close to the surface, as you will find if you go to the Parque Nacional Timanfaya, and much of the island is still covered with cindery *malpaís* (badlands). Fuerteventura has seen no volcanic activity for some 5,000 years, but has less rain than any of the islands, and the landscape is coloured in shades of brown and khaki, with great expanses of dunes.

Sculpture outside the Fundación César Manrique

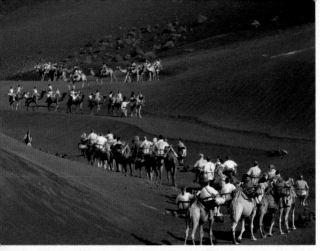

Camel trekking across the Parque Nacional Timanfaya's volcanic terrain

Lanzarote's highest point is Montaña Blanca, at 670 metres (2,198ft). The beaches around the major resorts, especially the famous ones at Puerto del Carmen, are covered with golden sands, as are the beautiful stretches close to Playa Blanca, while smaller, rockier coves retain their black volcanic sand. Of Fuerteventura's 152 beaches, some 50km (32 miles) consist of white sand, while about 25km (15 miles) are black volcanic shingle. The highest point on the island is Monte Jandía (807 metres/2,648ft).

The islands' average annual temperature is 20°C (68°F), with midsummer temperatures soaring to 28–30°C (82–86°F). Fuerteventura is usually windy – one explanation for the island's name is that it comes from *viento fuerte* (strong wind). On both islands, early mornings can be cloudy before blue skies and sunshine take over. There is little rain – what there is mostly falls between October and January. In summer the islands sometimes suffer from what is known as *tiempo Africano*

(African weather), when the hot sirocco wind sweeps up from the Sahara, covering the landscape with reddish dust.

Vegetation and Farming

There are few trees, apart fom the Canary palms *(Phoenix Canariensis)* in the Haría Valley, and those planted along the roadsides of many towns and resorts. Parks, hotel grounds and botanical gardens are bright with exotic plants brought to the island from southern Africa, South America and elsewhere that flourish happily in the islands' subtropical climate. The Strelitzia (bird-of-paradise flower) is one of the most showy, but hibiscus, poinsettia and agave are also common, and vividly coloured bougainvillea rampages over the garden walls and facades of villas and hotels.

Various forms of *Euphorbia* (spurge) flourish on the scrubby soil, including the *Euphorbia Canariensis* (candelabra spurge) and the rare, cactus-like *cardón de Jandía (Euphorbia handiensis),* found in the south of Fuerteventura.

A variety of prickly pear cactus cultivated mainly on Lanzarote is the nopal, on which the cochineal beetle feeds. When crushed, the beetle produces a red dye – cochineal. Although this is not the lucrative industry it was in the 19th century *(see page 17)*, a recent resurgence of interest in natural products means that cochineal is being produced in Lanzarote, but on a much smaller scale.

Another form of vegetation is that produced on the

On both islands you will see aloe vera, another cactus-like plant that has become very popular for medicinal and cosmetic purposes – especially to soothe sunburn – and is now being widely cultivated. The plant has long, greyish-green spiky leaves and spears of yellow flowers. You will find the products for sale in small shops, markets and supermarkets all over the islands.

Cacti flourish in the islands' dry, sandy soil

black lava called *picón*. This cinder, which collects and stores moisture from dew, is spread over arid soil and used for the cultivation of vines – especially in the La Geria region.

Wildlife

There is plenty for bird-watchers to spot on both islands during the winter months. Lanzarote's central plain is the best place to see Houbara bustards, kestrels, stone curlews and trumpeter finches – which are also found on Fuerteventura, along with the Fuerteventura chat. Berthelot's pipit can be seen all over the island, hoopoes are fairly common, and chiffchaffs and warblers are often found in urban settings. The Salinas de Janubio (salt pans) are a stopping-off place for many migratory birds, and numerous seabirds cluster on the offshore islands.

There are few mammals on either of the islands: bats, rats, mice, squirrels, rabbits and hedgehogs are about the sum of it. There are reptiles, though: geckos and lizards. The water around the islands is home to dolphins, porpoises and whales, and is rich in fish, including *corvina* (a kind of sea bass), *cherne* (wreckfish or stone bass), *sama* (sea bream) and *vieja* (parrot fish), as well as the more homely *sardinas* (sardines).

People and Language

The people of the Canary Islands have a strong sense of their identity as islanders and are keen to stress that they are *canarios* first and foremost. Spanish *(castellano)* is the language of the islands, but there are subtle differences from the peninsula, many of which reflect the two-way traffic between the Canaries and Latin America. Final consonants are swallowed and 'z' is pronounced 's', as in the Americas, rather than the lisped 'th' of mainland Spain. A number of Latino words have been borrowed, too: a bus is a *guagua* and potatoes are *papas*.

The Impact of Tourism

Traditionally, the islands' economy has been dependent on agriculture, but the principal source of revenue today comes from tourism. Lanzarote and Fuerteventura lack the loud nightlife and laddish culture that typifies parts of Tenerife and Gran Canaria. The strong winds and good waves attract surfing enthusiasts, but, apart from this, the equable climate means that the islands are all-round holiday destinations, with many older northern European visitors favouring the

Traditional costumes and music at a Lanzarote fiesta

cooler months as an escape from their own harsher winters, while families are in the majority during school holidays.

Obviously, the influx of tourists has had a major impact on the character of the islands, although Lanzarote has escaped the high-rise desecration that has spoiled parts of Tenerife and Gran Canaria. This is due in large part to the vision of artist César Manrique *(see page 25)*, who was influential in persuading the authorities to work with the island's landscape and natural features. Fuerteventura, which came later to tourism, has some rather characterless new resorts, but on the whole they are not badly done.

The resort of Caleta de Fuste on Fuerteventura

From volcanic landscapes to sandy beaches, the islands have much to offer, whether visitors are looking for water-sports or family entertainment, or are keen to discover the island way of life. The islands are easy to get around on well-surfaced roads, and there are some pleasant walking routes to suit people of all ages. While most accommodation is in purpose-built complexes, *turismo rural* has gained a foothold, making it possible to stay in rural properties in beautiful surroundings *(see page 126)* and sample traditional food. All in all, enough to convince most people that the islands merit one of their early names – the Fortunate Isles.

A BRIEF HISTORY

The Canary Islands have been part of Spain since they were conquered for the Spanish Crown in the late 15th century, but there was a flourishing culture here long before that, although no one is quite sure where the pre-Hispanic people came from. These early inhabitants are known collectively as the Guanches, although strictly speaking this was the name of a tribe that inhabited Tenerife. The people of Lanzarote and Fuerteventura prefer the name Majoreros, which is derived from Fuerteventura's indigenous name – Maxorata. Some historians think the original inhabitants were related to the Canarii people, who lived on the Saharan side of the Atlas Mountains. But as far as we know, the Guanches had no boats, so how they crossed from the African coast remains a mystery.

The Guanches were an agricultural people who mostly lived in groups of caves, but on the three eastern islands they also built houses. On Lanzarote and Fuerteventura their dwellings were grouped into hamlets around the edges of lava fields. Their society had a hierarchical structure, with kings – *guanartemes* – and priests – *faycans*. Lanzarote was a single kingdom, but on Fuerteventura there were two – Maxorata in the north and Jandía in the south, beyond La Pared, the wall that once stretched across the narrowest part of the island. These early people mummified their dead and buried them in caves or stone-lined graves, and it is evidence from mummies that has led scientists to place the islanders' ethnic origins in northwest Africa.

The Guanches (or Majoreros) did not have the wheel, they knew nothing of metalworking and did not use bows and arrows – their main weapons were wooden spears. Domestic implements were made from stone and bone or from obsidian, a black, volcanic glass. Porous lava was made into millstones

Scientist and explorer Alexander von Humboldt, who visited Lanzarote in 1799 en route to South America, claimed the indigenous people had an unusual custom: 'A woman had several husbands, who each took it in turn to exercise the rights of the head of the family. Each husband was known as such during a lunar month; then another took his place while he returned to being a servant in the house.'

and mortars. Their vessels and containers were made from pottery, wood, leather and woven cane. *Gofio*, toasted flour originally made from barley, was their staple food, but they also ate a variety of roots, wild fruits and berries. Pigs, sheep and goats provided meat as well as the materials for shelters, containers and clothes, and milk also came from sheep and goats. Fish formed a part of their diet, even when they had to travel some distance down to the coast to find it.

Arrival of the Europeans

The first documented account of a European expedition to the Canary Islands was in 1339, when the Genoese Lanzarotto Malocello discovered the island that was named after him. The first detailed description of the islands was written two years later by Genoese historian Nicoloso da Recco, who accompanied a slave-traders' voyage, of which he wrote: 'The natives of Fuerteventura are few in number and live on meat and milk, and are of great stature, and are very firm in their beliefs.' Various expeditions were mounted during the course of the century, but it was not until 1402 that the first conquerors arrived. Jean de Béthencourt and Gadifer de la Salle, Norman noblemen who had pledged allegiance to the king of Castile, claimed Lanzarote, Fuerteventura and El Hierro for their royal master, although they failed to take Gran Canaria and Tenerife. As was usually the case with conquerors, they claimed the expedition was 'for the exaltation of the Christian faith', so they must have been delighted when the last king of Lanzarote, after several failed escape attempts, finally agreed to Christian baptism.

Many of the indigenous people were sold into slavery and many more died of European diseases, but those who survived intermarried with the colonisers, who settled down to a harsh life, making their living from the land and sea.

It wasn't until 1478 that another attempt was made to conquer the larger islands, under the aegis of the Catholic Monarchs – Ferdinand and Isabella – of a newly united Spain. It took several years to subdue the indigenous people, but eventually all of the Canary Islands became Spanish possessions.

Jean de Béthencourt

Because of their location, the islands were vital for Spanish colonisation in the Americas. This revolved around slavery and sugar cane, both of which were introduced to the Americas from the Canaries, but it was Gran Canaria and Tenerife which were the main beneficiaries. Of no interest to their Spanish masters and with little source of income, many inhabitants of Lanzarote and Fuerteventura turned to piracy during the 16th and early 17th centuries, a somewhat precarious way of earning a living, and one that laid them open to reciprocal attacks.

Explosive Events

In the mid-18th century, memories of pirate raids faded into insignificance when Lanzarote experienced a devastating series of volcanic eruptions. In 1730, Timanfaya erupted, and continued to pour molten lava and black ash down its slopes for a further six years, until a third of the island had been devastated, many of its inhabitants had fled to Gran Canaria and some had set out on the long journey to Latin America. For almost a century the volcano appeared to sleep, but 1824 saw another series of eruptions, albeit smaller ones. Visitors to the dark, eerie landscape now protected as the Parque Nacional de Timanfaya may be able to visualise the devastation.

Although the eruptions overwhelmed the most fertile part of the island, the volcanic ash formed *picón*, dark cinders that collect and retain the dew, forming a natural irrigation system. On this the islanders were able to grow a variety of vegetables, and to profit from the cultivation of vines and export of wine – a prosperous period that lasted until the early 19th century. This system, known as *enarenad*, was later practised in arid parts of the Spanish mainland, although silicon sand was used instead of cinder. The next money-spinner was cochineal, a red dye created by crushing the beetle *(Dactylopius coccus costa)* that fed on the nopal cactus, and which was introduced to the islands in around 1825. For some 50 years the in-

> The parish priest of Yaiza, Andrés Lorenzo Curbelo, described the 1730 eruption as 'an enormous mountain that rose out of the bosom of the earth. From its flat top flames belched out and continued burning for 19 days.' Several months later 'new eruptions came... [with] incandescent streams of lava, together with the densest smoke.'

Volcanic landscape formed by the eruptions of Timanfaya

dustry flourished, before the creation of aniline dyes made it largely superfluous.

During the latter part of this period the larger, more powerful islands of Gran Canaria and Tenerife were flexing their muscles, demanding a degree of independence from Spain and vying with each other for supremacy at the same time. Tenerife, which had profited from the wine trade (Gran Canaria's soil was unsuitable for viniculture) and other long-distance commerce was by far the wealthier and had established a university in the town of La Laguna, which became an intellectual centre. Gran Canaria resented Tenerife's powerful position and, under the late 19th-century leadership of Fernando León y Castillo, foreign minister in the national government, made a bid for supremacy. In 1903, emboldened by Cuba gaining freedom from Spain five years earlier, the Partido Local Canario was formed, with the aim of achieving some degree of independence and dividing the archipelago into two provinces. This was formalised in 1927, but brought little economic relief to the islands, whose trade had been badly hit by World War I and its economic aftermath. Lanzarote and Fuerteventura became part of the Eastern Province, governed, as they are today, from Las Palmas de Gran Canaria. The seat of island government (Cabildo Insular) alternates between Las Palmas and Santa Cruz de Tenerife every four years.

There had been a gradual flow of people from the Canaries to the Americas since the late 16th century, but agricultural decline in the late 19th and early 20th centuries accentuated this traffic, as people went looking for a better way of life. Remittances were sent home, and many of those who made good returned to the islands and built homes or established small businesses, thus accentuating the ties with Latin America that are still apparent today. You can visit

Many *canarios* emigrated to the Americas in search of a better life

the Museo del Emigrante just outside Teguise (Lanzarote) to learn more about this *(see page 46)*.

(see page 46).

> **Fidel Castro expressed his admiration for Canarian emigrants to Cuba, who 'helped forge the country with their proverbial hard work'. From them, he said, 'our peasants inherited their seriousness, their decency, their sense of honour and also their rebelliousness.'**

Political Upheavals

In 1924, under the dictatorship of Miguel Primo de Rivera, Fuerteventura, the bleakest of the Canary Islands, was judged a suitable place to send political dissidents. Writer and philosopher Miguel de Unamuno was the best known of these. He came to love the island, which he described as 'a rock thirsting in the sun, a treasure of health and honesty'. There is a monument to him in the north of the island.

In 1936, the three-year Spanish Civil War began, initiated by Francisco Franco, military governor of the Canary Islands. He spent the last night before launching his coup in the Hotel Madrid in Las Palmas.

After the bitter Civil War and World War II, the Canaries, like the rest of Spain, initially suffered from political isolation and economic hardship. Things improved a little in the 1950s, when Spain was once more recognised by the international community, but it was the advent of tourism in the following decade that really turned the tide.

Franco remained in power until his death in 1975, when his authoritarian regime was replaced by democratic government. The new Spanish Constitution of 1978 created the Autonomous Region of the Canary Islands – now one of 17 such regions. The archipelago is not completely separate from Spain, but the island government, known as the Cabildo Insular, does have a great deal of freedom. In the

A young islander looks to the future

national elections of 1996, the Coalición Canaria, a union of regional parties, took four seats in the Madrid parliament (this was reduced to three in the 2004 elections) and now sees its role as working with the national government to win improvements for the islands, rather than looking for further independence. This is not to say that no resentment is felt towards Madrid, but resentment of central government is, perhaps, a fact of life wherever regional feelings are strong.

Many mainland Spaniards, particularly from the poorer regions – Andalusia and Galicia – are to be found working in the islands' service industries. They have integrated well into island life and, while there is some dissatisfaction expressed about them doing jobs that might be done by local people, there is relatively little ill-feeling.

The islands have enjoyed considerable commercial freedom and tax exemptions ever since the 19th century. When

Spain became a full member of the European Union, fiscal changes had to be introduced, but important tax privileges were negotiated. Motorists will be pleased to find that the islands still have the cheapest petrol in Europe.

Tourism, Economy and Environment

Traditionally, the economy of the islands has been dependent on agriculture and fishing, but the principal source of employment and revenue today is in the service sector, of which tourism is a major part. Some 90 percent of Lanzarote's inhabitants work in the tourist industry and the infrastructure that supports it, and the percentage in Fuerteventura is similar. When Arrecife airport opened in the early 1960s (it was refurbished and extended in 1999 to cope with the large number of passengers), tourism started to take off. Fuerteventura's airport opened in 1969, and while the growth of the tourist industry was slower here than on the other islands, it has increased in recent years. Lanzarote now receives about 1.8 million visitors annually, Fuerteventura some 1.5 million, mainly English, Germans and Scandinavians, as well as visitors from mainland Spain. There are

Dangerous Journeys

Lanzarote and Fuerteventura have become the main route into Europe for illegal immigrants from Africa. Now that strict controls have made it virtually impossible for them to cross from northern Morocco to southern Spain, desperate people board small fishing boats near Layooune, the capital of Moroccan-occupied Western Sahara, paying around €500 (£350) each, to make the dangerous journey to these islands, which are the closest to the African coast. Many drown, or die of dehydration, during the course of their journey. Others reach the island shores to face an uncertain future.

believed to be around 50,000 foreign property owners on Lanzarote, and some have established bars, clubs and other small businesses. There are fewer home owners on Fuerteventura, but numbers are rising.

The eastern islands suffer from severe water shortage (they receive less rainfall than parts of the Sahara), a problem intensified by the strain that so many visitors place on the system. Although this has been partly overcome by the creation of desalination plants, visitors should try to be frugal in their use of water, although in hot summer weather it can be rather difficult.

The islands utilise their strong winds, as they always have

The availability of work in the tourist industry has also encouraged many young people to desert the land and the fishing industry (although Arrecife still has the biggest fishing fleet in the Canaries) in favour of finding higher wages and more fun in the resorts. But life for the islanders has rarely been easy, and it is understandable that the latest generation should look for alternatives. Most people believe that tourism has brought more advantages than disadvantages to the islands, and that the inhabitants' individuality and love of their lands will enable them to retain their special character, despite the many changes.

Historical Landmarks

*c.*2nd–1st centuries BC Settlements of Guanches – or Majoreros – in Canary Islands.

AD1339 Genoese Lanzarotto Malocello discovers Lanzarote.

1402 Jean de Béthencourt and Gadifer de la Salle invade and claim Lanzarote, Fuerteventura and El Hierro.

1478–83 Canary Islands brought under control of Spanish Crown.

16th–17th centuries Many inhabitants of impoverished Lanzarote and Fuerteventura turn to piracy.

1730–6 Continuous eruptions of Mount Timanfaya; a third of Lanzarote is devastated.

1730–1950 Poverty forces widespread emigration to Latin America.

1825–75 Economic boom follows the introduction of the cochineal beetle, but the industry is ruined by the invention of aniline dyes.

1852 Isabella II declares the Canary Islands a Free Trade Zone.

1911 Self-administration council – Cabildo Insular – introduced.

1927 Canary Islands are divided in two. Lanzarote and Fuerteventura become part of the Eastern Province, governed from Gran Canaria.

1936 Franco initiates the three-year Spanish Civil War.

1962 Lanzarote's Arrecife airport opens. Tourism rapidly develops into the most important industry.

1969 Fuerteventura airport opens. Tourism develops more slowly here.

1970s Influenced by artist and architect César Manrique, the Cabildo imposes strict building regulations on Lanzarote.

1978–82 Spanish Constitution joins the two island provinces to form the Autonomous Region of the Canary Islands.

1986 Spain joins the EU and negotiates special status for the Canaries.

1995 Islands integrated into the EU but retain important tax privileges.

2002 The euro becomes the national currency.

2004 In national elections, the Coalición Canaria wins three seats in the Madrid parliament (one fewer than in 1996).

2005–6 Lanzarote receives about 1.8 million visitors annually, Fuerteventura some 1.5 million.

LANZAROTE

Lanzarote is a small island, but it packs a lot of contrasts into a limited space. From the awesome, unearthly Montañas del Fuego in the Parque Nacional de Timanfaya to the verdant 'Valley of a Thousand Palms' around Haría; from the tranquillity of Isla Graciosa to the razzmatazz of Puerto del Carmen, there is always something to surprise the visitor. One thing is consistent, however: the building limits proposed by artist César Manrique and imposed by the island government have ensured that, with a few exceptions, the architecture consists of low white buildings with green, blue or brown balconies and shutters, which complement the indigenous architecture of the island.

Lanzarote is an easy place to get around. For the sake of simplicity this guide starts with the capital, Arrecife, then divides the island into three areas: north, south and centre. However, distances are so small that you may well find yourself straying from one region to the other on a single trip. Just follow your own whims and instincts and you won't go far wrong.

ARRECIFE

Arrecife lies 8km (5 miles) east of the airport, from where it is well served by inexpensive taxis. Buses *(guaguas)* run every 20 minutes to Costa Teguise and Puerto del Carmen, and taxi fares to both resorts are very reasonable, too. The town has a long history, as its two small sturdy fortresses demonstrate. Castillo de San Gabriel was built in the second half of the 17th century to reinforce the town against attacks from the sea; it was the work of Genoese engineer Leonardo Torriani, who was also responsible for the Castillo de Santa

One of Playa Blanca's inviting beaches

Bárbara in Teguise. The Castillo de San José dates from about a century later, when pirate attacks were still a problem. It was also a work-creation project, as the people of Lanzarote were suffering great poverty following periods of drought and the eruption of Timanfaya, which had destroyed farmland in the most fertile part of the island. For a long time it was known as the Castillo del Hambre (Fortress of Hunger). In 1852, when piracy had ceased to be a threat, Arrecife took over from Teguise as the capital of Lanzarote. By this time, links with Spain's American colonies meant that it made more sense to have a capital on the coast.

Arrecife is a down-to-earth, working city, home to about half the island's population. It has few buildings of architectural interest and not a great deal in the way of culture, but it is well worth a visit if you want to see a slice of island life, away from the resorts or the picture-postcard villages. It has a few decent tapas bars, an excellent restaurant in the Castillo de San José, food to be purchased in the market and local shops that is far more varied and much cheaper than in the resorts, and an excellent curved beach – Playa Reducto – with golden sands and calm, safe waters. If you want a quiet holiday there is a lot to be said for making a base here in one of the seafront hotels.

The Charco de San Ginés

Exploring the Town

If you are come into Arrecife by car, get off the *circun-valación* (ring road) at the west (airport) end of town, and you will be able to leave your car in a large, free car park at the end of the beach, opposite the smart new Cabildo Insular building, and thereby avoid the narrow streets and one-way system of the city. Looming at the

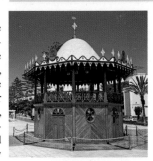

Kiosko de la Música

other end of the beach is the 17-storey **Gran Hotel** (which has a large underground car park). This was the building that so upset Manrique when he returned to the island from New York that he took steps to ensure that Lanzarote's skyline would not become disfigured by similar high-rises. The hotel was gutted by fire in 1994 and remained empty for years but has now re-opened. Although it breaks all the rules, it is a sleek, well-designed building. You can take the glass lift to the top, where a there's a restaurant and a café that offers views over the town and down to Puerto del Carmen – and good coffee and cake.

Newly planted gardens and a wooden walkway lead towards the town centre. On a corner, opposite an attractive Canarian-style building belonging to the Cabildo, old men sit in a little square playing dominoes. A broad promenade runs east from here. The statue at the beginning is of Blas Cabrera Felipe (1878–1945), an eminent scientist who was born in the town. There are seats in flower-decked bowers, and egrets squawk and flap in the palm trees. Housed in a circular wooden kiosk called the **Kiosko de la Música**, where a band sometimes plays, is the tourist office (Mon–Fri 9.30am–1.30pm, 4.30–7pm, Sat 9.30am–1.30pm). Staff are friendly

Guarding Castillo de San Gabriel

and will give you leaflets and town plans but not a lot of information. On the other side of the road (now the Avenida de la Marina, although some maps still show it as Avenida General Franco) is the post office and the Casa de Cultura, which houses a museum (closed for renovation).

Cross a little bridge to the **Castillo de San Gabriel** (Tues–Fri 10am–1pm, 4–7pm; free), with a rusty cannon standing outside. The little fortress used to house an archaeological museum, but these days it just outlines the history of piracy in a series of tiny, thick-walled rooms, and will not detain you for long. You can cross back to the seafront via a parallel bridge, the **Puente de las Bolas**, named for the cannon balls atop its twin pillars. Follow the promenade (now called Avenida Coll) a short way to the right (towards the port), passing the Ayuntamiento (Town Hall), then cross the road to the **Charco de San Ginés**. This pretty little tidal lagoon, where boats bob serenely on the water, is surrounded by brightly shuttered buildings, several of which house restaurants. The only incongruous feature is a large, four-screen cinema – but local people are probably glad of the entertainment.

You can walk all the way round the lagoon then off into the town to the Plaza de las Palmas, and the parish church, the **Iglesia de San Ginés** (daily 9am–1pm, 4–7pm), with a distinctive white cupola topping its bell tower. It is dedicated to the town's patron saint, whose festival is celebrated here in August. There is a simple interior, with a good *mudéjar* ceiling of dark wood. If you find the church closed (the opening hours are not to be relied on), just sit on one of the benches in the shady square, listen to the drip of a central fountain and admire the exterior of the building.

Narrow lanes lead from the square into the centre of the town, focused on the pedestrianised shopping street, **Calle León y Castillo**, running back from the seafront. Here, branches of well-known stores such as Zara and Mango share space with the large HiperDino supermarket and a few delightfully old-fashioned shops such as the Almacenes Arencibia, with shirts and jerseys stacked neatly on glass-fronted wooden shelves.

Art in Arrecife

Go west, via the oblong Plaza de la Constitución, where there are a couple of tapas bars with seats outside in the square, to-wards Calle Betancort. Here you will find **El Almacén** (daily 10am–7pm), a cultural centre in an old store converted by

León y Castillo

You may wonder why most towns and villages in Lanzarote have a street or square called León y Castillo. This has nothing to do with lions or castles, but pays homage to two brothers, Fernando and Juan, who were born in Telde, Gran Canaria, where there is now a museum devoted to them. Fernando, who became foreign minister in the Spanish government in 1881, implemented a programme of improvements to the port of Las Palmas, the plans for which were drawn up by his engineer brother Juan. This made it the major port in the archipelago and an important stop on the new steamship route to the West Indies, and changed the ailing fortunes of Gran Canaria and, by extension, of Lanzarote and Fuerteventura.

Castillo de San José

César Manrique. The centre includes the Bar Picasso (open until late) where there is sometimes live music, two galleries with changing exhibitions (although there may be periods when nothing is on) and, on the top floor, the Cine Buñuel, which shows art house films.

Arrecife is a small town, and all of the above can easily be done on foot, but to visit the last place of interest you need to take a taxi. They are readily available, and it should cost no more than €3 from the centre to the **Castillo de San José**, which houses the **Museo Internacional de Arte Contemporáneo** (daily 11am–9pm; free). The fortress had fallen into disrepair by the 20th century, and in 1975 Manrique directed the renovation of the building and founded the Museum of Contemporary Art. In a series of cool rooms within the thick stone walls is a collection of paintings, sketches and sculpture by internationally known artists such as Antoni Tàpies, as well as Manrique himself and other renowned Canarian artists. Down a flight of stairs more paintings decorate the walls of a restaurant and bar (daily; restaurant 1–3.45pm, 7.30–11pm; bar 11am–midnight). From the floor-to-ceiling windows there is a view of the port – not traditionally picturesque, but in this context the cranes and containers have a sculptural beauty. You can eat very well here *(see page 134)*, or just enjoy the view from a low, comfy bar stool while you have a drink – and bar prices are surprisingly low for such a smart venue.

THE NORTH

The north of the island is a treasure trove of natural wonders and man-made attractions. Nature has given us the dramatic cliffs of Risco de Famara on the west coast, the *malpaís* (badlands) on the east, the fascinating Cueva de los Verdes and the tranquil island of Isla Graciosa, while man (or, to be specific, Manrique) has created the breathtaking Jameos del Agua, the Jardín de Cactus and the Mirador del Río.

Jardín de Cactus and Arrieta

From the *circunvalación* around Arrecife, take the LZ1 north towards **Guatiza** to visit the **Jardín de Cactus** (daily 10am–5.45pm; admission fee includes a drink in the café). As you enter Guatiza you pass fields of cultivated cactus, for this is the region of Lanzarote where cochineal is still produced, albeit not in large quantities *(see page 16)*. Set in a volcanic crater, this Manrique-designed garden spirals in a circle of terraces up to a small windmill. There are cacti of all kinds: round and dumpy, tall and phallic, and some like little furry creatures snuggled in the volcanic soil. Manrique's designs on the external walls of the toilets are attractions in themselves.

Jardín de Cactus

A strange house stands on one of Arrieta's jetties, pagoda-like in bright blue and brick-red. The building has a sad story to tell: in the 1920s a local man emigrated to Argentina, where he prospered, but his young daughter fell gravely ill and he was advised that the Atlantic winds would be good for her. He returned and built a house as exposed to the elements as possible in a style popular in Argentina at the time. Sadly, the daughter died, despite his care, and is buried in the local cemetery.

On the way between Guatiza and the next destination, the Jameos del Agua, you could make a brief detour to **Arrieta**. We are definitely in Manrique country here, and one of his sculptures, like a giant wind chime, stands at a roundabout where a road leads the short distance to the coast and this tiny fishing village. To the right, before you enter the village, you could turn off to the pleasant **Playa de la Garita**. Arrieta is a sleepy place, although quite popular with divers, and it gets animated at weekend lunchtimes when several fish restaurants around the small harbour draw customers.

Jameos del Agua and Cueva de los Verdes

Continue north for about 3km (2 miles) to the well-signposted **Jameos del Agua** (daily 10am–6.30pm; bar 10am–6.30pm and 7pm–2am; restaurant Tues, Fri–Sat also 7.30–11.30pm; admission fee). You turn off onto a road that is in many places not wide enough for two-way traffic, but there are many passing places, and people are usually courteous about using them. This is one site that just about everybody comes to, so it can get busy – try to come fairly early, or at the end of the day – and it is like nothing else you will ever have seen. It is part of volcanic tunnel system that runs from Montaña de Corona, which erupted about 4,000 years ago, out into the

Atlantic. It was this eruption that created the *malpaís* (now a protected area) through which you will drive if you continue north. A *jameo* is the name for a cavity produced when the roof of a volcanic tunnel collapses.

Within this one, Manrique created an extraordinary underground world. You go down steps to the *jameo chico* (small cave) to a bar/restaurant, full of lush foliage and soft music, from where narrow paths lead to a saltwater lake of varying depth depending on the tide. The lake is home to a unique variety of crab *(Munidopsis polymorpha)*, white, blind and without shells – as they have no predators, they had no need to develop them. Notices around the lake (and on your ticket) tell you that it is forbidden to throw coins into the water, as their corrosion would endanger the crabs. At the other side of the lake, landscaped terraces lead up to ground level. At the far side is a 600-seat auditorium, with splendid acoustics, which

Jameos del Agua

Cueva de los Verdes

has been closed for renovation for some years but is due to reopen for musical performances by the end of 2007.

About 1km (½ mile) up a narrow road opposite lies the **Cueva de los Verdes** (daily 10am–5pm; guided tour; admission fee). *Verde* means green, but the name refers not to the colour of the rocks but to a family called Verde who used to keep their goats in the upper part of the cave. Over the years, these caverns served as a place of refuge for local people when pirates attacked the shores. The cave system is part of the same 'tube' that runs from Montaña de Corona to the sea.

You may have to wait a short while to go in, as the numbers on each tour are limited, but they run very frequently and last about 50 minutes. The temperature inside the caves remains stable at 18–20°C (64–68°F) throughout the year, which makes the visit a pleasant escape from summer heat. Claustrophobics should be all right, as, after an initial low, narrow stretch, the cave opens out into a vast cavern, and thereafter there are few places where you need to stoop. The tour does involve shuffling along rather slowly, however – how slowly depends on the composition of your group and how many people linger to take photos. It's worth the shuffle, though, as the shapes of the cave walls and ceilings, formed by the solidified lava and enhanced by discreet lighting, are quite extraordinary. Your guide will lead you into an auditorium, where concerts are sometimes held, as the acoustics are excellent.

Presumably only small, portable instruments can be used. As the tour draws to an end, the guide will demand silence in order to introduce you to the 'secret of the caves' – it's an ingenious one, and we are not going to give the game away.

Mirador del Río and Parque Tropical

Continue northwards, through cindery *malpaís*, where only lichen-covered rocks and euphorbia bushes enliven the black terrain. After a while a few small vineyards appear, the vines planted in the traditional Lanzarote way, within a semicircle of rocks *(see page 49)*. On a hillside, a bodega offers tastings and sells wine. The road ends at the **Mirador del Río** (daily 10am–5.45pm; admission fee includes a drink in the bar). You will not be surprised to learn that it was Manrique who transformed this disused gun emplacement into a lookout point and glass-fronted café. The views are stupendous, encompassing

Looking out from the Mirador del Río

Isla Graciosa *(see page 37)*, with the smaller islands of Montaña Clara and Alegranza in the distance. The stretch of water separating Graciosa from the mainland is called a *río* (river) but is, in fact, a narrow channel in the Atlantic.

A clifftop stretch of road leads along the Risco de Famara (cliffs), then to lower ground. The views are wonderful, but don't stop to enjoy them until you find a suitable place, as the road is very narrow. You pass the oddly named little village of Yé before reaching the **Parque Tropical** (daily 10am–5pm; admission charge) at **Guinate**. This is a great family outing, although, at €14 (€5 for children), it ought to be.

As well as clearly described subtropical plants and a big cactus garden, there is a vast number of exotic birds (the owners claim 1,300), plus a few monkeys rescued from illegal ownership, and the ever-popular meerkats. Those who object strongly to keeping birds in captivity will, of course, give it a miss, but the conditions are good. There is a large walk-through aviary, and the cages otherwise are huge and well furnished with plants, and appear to offer the birds all the freedom they need – except the freedom to fly away, of course. Parrot shows are held at intervals throughout the day, and there is a café with reasonably priced snacks and light meals.

Spick and span Haría

Haría

Continuing south, you drop down into the greenest, most fertile part of the island, the valley of **Haría**, known as the ◀ 'Valley of a Thousand Palms'. This is an exaggeration, but there are quite a lot of them. As tour guides and brochures are keen to point out, the legend recounts that once upon a time a palm tree was planted for every girl born locally, and two for every boy. Haría is a nice little town (although a place of confusing road signs). Spick and span in white and green, it has attracted a number of artists and artisans in its time, and became Manrique's home during his later years. The church, **Nuestra Señora de la Encarnación**, is a modern copy of the 17th-century original which was damaged by a storm, then destroyed, in the 1950s. There's a good **craft market** in the square around the church (Plaza de León y Castillo) every Saturday. Much of the work on sale is made at the **Centro de Artesanía** (daily 10am–1.30pm, 4–7pm; free), a craft-workers' co-operative.

Órzola and Isla Graciosa

At the tip of the island, with its back to the badlands, lies the village of **Órzola**, jumping-off point for Isla Graciosa. There's not much to Órzola, apart from a number of good fish restaurants *(see pages 136)*, from the terraces of which you can watch the comings and goings of boats to the island *(see page 83 for details)*. The trip to **Isla Graciosa** takes ◀ about 20 minutes, but it leads you into another world. Part of the protected **Parque Natural del Archipélago Chinijo**, it has only one settlement, Caleta del Sebo, and a population of 630. There are no cars, except a

There are car parks just inland from Órzola harbour; the bays directly in front of it only allow you to park for 2½ hours – no good if you're going to the island.

A daredevil goat at Las Pardelas

few Land Rovers and, apart from the *paseo* around the harbour, no paved roads. To get around, you have to walk, or hire a bike, which is easily done from a couple of outlets by the port. There are several fish restaurants around the harbour and in the streets behind it, but if you come on a weekday they may not all be open. Most people buy picnic supplies from one of three little supermarkets and head for the beaches. There's a small golden beach and protected waters right by the harbour where local children splash about, but the better beaches are a little way away. The currents are very strong, so swimming is not a good idea. Paddle instead, and explore the rock pools where tiny fish swim around your feet.

If you are back at the harbour around 3pm you'll see the fishing smacks come in, and you can watch as small fish are unloaded from the decks into wheelbarrows and taken a few yards away to be laid out on the jetty to dry in the sun. These are *pejines*; when dried, they are grilled and eaten as tapas.

Back on the mainland, going south from Órzola, the best route is along the coast, but there is a narrow lane out of the village that takes you back to the main Arrieta to Mirador del Río road, and a short way up the lane is **Las Pardelas** (daily 10am–6pm; admission fee). This friendly, family-run little ecological park with indigenous plants, domestic animals and donkey rides has a small restaurant, and makes a nice gentle stop if you are travelling with children.

THE CENTRE

The centre of the island is where you will find the airport, the capital, Arrecife, the two largest resorts, Puerto del Carmen and Costa de Teguise, the historic town of Teguise, a number of interesting rural museums, the wine-producing zone and the stunning Fundación César Manrique in the artist's home.

Costa Teguise

Costa Teguise is the only resort north of Arrecife. You enter on the Avenida del Mar (about 14km/8 miles from the airport, 6km/4 miles from the capital), a broad road lined with squat palm trees and flanked by apartment blocks and hotels. The main street, Avenida de las Islas Canarias, running parallel to the coast, is lined with commercial centres, small supermarkets, several clinics and a plethora of car-hire outlets.

Playa de las Cucharas, Costa Teguise

Building materials and paint for external surfaces in Lanzarote are only available in brown, green and blue, the designated colours for woodwork on the white buildings.

Manrique designed the **Pueblo Marinero** at the southern end of the resort, and this is the most appealing part of the development. Low, whitewashed houses with blue or green balconies are clustered in narrow streets around a small square, and it does genuinely resemble a fishing village – which is what Pueblo Marinero means. Later construction, running down to the beach, was taken over by other, less purist hands. A clutch of restaurants and bars here offer fish and chips, hamburgers and pizza, and many have English names – including The Sunburnt Arms. Round the rocky headland there are more buildings going up, and there's a small beach, **Playa del Jablillo**, with a rather unlovely view of the desalination plant just outside Arrecife.

Running northwards, the **Playa de las Cucharas** and **Playa de los Charcos** merge. The former has the better beach, a long stretch of golden imported sand superimposed on the natural volcanic black, and a stretch that is popular with windsurfers, as the winds on this coast are often strong. There is sand on Playa de los Charcos, too, but here there are black rocks to clamber over between the sand and the sea.

A landscaped promenade runs the length of the beaches, with a scattering of cafés and restaurants, and passes the smart Hotel Meliá Salinas, designed by Manrique, which in the 1970s became the first to be built here. The early ambitions for Costa Teguise have not been realised; it lacks a real heart and is more downmarket than the other two major resorts. As a base for exploring the island, however, it has its advantages, as it is very convenient for visiting the cultural sites and villages in the north and centre of Lanzarote.

Fundación César Manrique

From the *circunvalación* around Arrecife the LZ1 leads some 5km (3 miles) to **Tahiche**, where, on the outskirts, you will find the **Fundación César Manrique** (Jul–Oct Mon–Sat 10am–7pm; Nov–Jun Mon–Sat 10am–6pm, Sun 10am–3pm; admission fee). This was the artist's home, which he remodelled as a museum and gallery when creating the foundation in 1982. All is white: outside, paths and walls gleam like icing sugar on a cake; inside, the marble floors blend with the white walls. Huge windows give views over the surrounding landscape, where the coils of molten lava look as if they might still be liquid. The exhibition salons contain Manrique's own paintings, ceramics and sketches, as well as works by Picasso, Tàpies and Miró. Steps lead down to a series of volcanic bubbles, where trees reach up for the light. A subterranean garden has a pool and retains the atmosphere

Manrique's abstract mural at the Fundación

of a private home, with a huge barbecue and benches built into the walls. As you leave the building you pass through a small garden with a central pond and fountain, and a huge abstract mural that is one of Lanzarote's iconic sights.

Rural Heartland

About 8km (5 miles) west of the foundation you come to the sleepy little town of **San Bartolomé**. The parish church (often closed), the Teatro Municipal and the Ayuntamiento (Town Hall) form two sides of an attractive square with a colonnade, palm trees and a central fountain. Opposite, an open-ended plaza, planted with palms, cacti and oleanders, leads, via broad steps, down to the **Museo Tanit** (Mon–Sat 10am–2pm; admission fee), an ethnographic museum that outlines the history of the island's earliest inhabitants and has displays on island life during the past two centuries.

A right turn from the outskirts of San Bartolomé takes you the short distance to **Mozaga** and the **Monumento del Campesino** (Monument to the Countryman), which is set in the exact centre of the island. Manrique's huge white sculpture depicts the *campesino*, surrounded, on the four compass points, by a camel, a donkey, a dog and a goat – although the abstract nature of the construction means that you need a bit of imagination to discern their figures.

Beside the monument a collection of attractive white buildings with green shutters comprise a bar and restaurant and the **Centro de Artesanía** (although signs on the road outside call it the 'Casa-Museo Manrique'). You can skirt the restaurant to reach the artisans' centre, but don't – if you enter via the huge, domed structure you go through a rocky tunnel and a cool grotto to reach your destination. On the ground floor around a square are workshops where demonstrations of weaving, leather-working and pottery take place. Upstairs a small museum displays models of Lanzarote's early *ermitas* (chapels) and some excellent naive ceramic works portraying primitive figures grinding and milling wheat.

The road leads north from the monument towards Tigua. On the far side of the village you come to a tiny white *ermita*, and a right turn leads to the **Museo Agrícola El Patio** (Mon–Fri 10am–5.30pm, Sat 10am–2.30pm; admission fee). A museum of agriculture might not be your first idea of fun, but this one is a delight. On a small estate, once a rural centre where corn was brought to be milled, a fascinating collection of agricultural and domestic objects (complete with some spooky figures, their faces made from gourds) has been gathered. Set in grounds where chicken scratch in the dust and a donkey, goat and camel keep the farmyard theme alive, the museum is housed in a *finca* (farmhouse) dating from 1840 and a large converted barn. Perhaps the most interesting of the displays are numerous old photos, dating from the early

Remnants of a bygone age in El Patio Museum

years of the 20th century to the 1960s, depicting the hardships and the community spirit of rural life. Leaving the museum, you pass through the old bodega, where you will be offered a glass of local wine. A quotation on one of the museum walls by Tenerife-born writer Agustín Espinosa (1897–1939) reads: 'A land without traditions, without a poetic atmosphere, faces the threat of extinction.' This place is doing all it can to keep those traditions and atmosphere alive.

Teguise

Teguise was the first colonial capital of the island, built in the centre in the hope that it would be safe from pirate attacks. As you will learn if you visit the Castillo de Santa Bárbara *(see page 46)*, this was not the case, but 'the royal town', as it was known, remained the capital until 1852. It is an attractive place, a village more than a town, with cobbled streets and a number of well-restored colonial buildings with typical Canarian-style wooden balconies and pretty courtyards.

Sunday is **market day** in Teguise, and tourists from all over the island descend on the little town – coach tours run from all the resorts. If you come by car, a series of car parks on the approach to town make life easy; attendants collect a fee of €1.50. The market sprawls all over Teguise, and there's a lively atmosphere, although you won't find much that you couldn't get in tourist shops and markets in any resort in Europe. Even the food on sale in the stalls and kiosks tends towards hamburgers, doughnuts and pizza rather than anything local. There are several good restaurants, though, where you can find Canarian food *(see page 138),* and a number of shops

> **Teguise has a very lively carnival in February or early March, in which characters dressed as devils and brandishing goatskin truncheons attempt to terrorise carnival revellers.**

with more interesting goods: aloe vera products of all kinds are sold in several places, as are local cheeses, wine and jars of *mojo* sauce, and a few ceramics and woven goods, as well as an outlet of the Manrique Foundation. Around midday there is a 30-minute exhibition of *lucha canaria (see page 80)* in a domed structure in the village centre. Wine-and-cheese tasting are included in the ticket price.

There are three impressive churches in Teguise, two of them monastic, but, despite the information in some tourist-office leaflets, you may not find them open.

The popular market at Teguise

The **Convento de Santo Domingo**, founded by the Dominican Order in 1698, is now an art centre, which holds exhibitions of contemporary work. When there is an exhibition on, the building is open Mon–Fri 10am–3pm; otherwise you cannot gain access. The church is worth a look if you can get in: it has two naves, and the chapel dedicated to the Virgen del Rosario is the only one in Lanzarote where the retrochoir (the area directly behind the altar) features painted murals.

The **Convento de San Francisco**, founded by Franciscans in the late 16th century, houses a museum of sacred art, but has been closed for some time. Enquire when you visit if it has reopened; otherwise you will have to be content with admiring the splendid main doorway. The **Iglesia de Nuestra**

Convento de San Francisco

Señora de Guadalupe is an eclectic mixture of styles, having been remodelled many times during its long history, following pirate attacks and fires. Again, you may not find it open, but do not despair – Teguise has some great domestic architecture. The **Casa-Museo Palacio Spínola** (Mon–Fri 9am–4pm, Sat–Sun 9am–3pm; admission fee) is a delight. Built in the mid-18th century by an aristocratic family, it was restored in the 1970s, purchased by the local authorities and in 1989 became the official residence of the Canary Islands Autonomous Government. A series of beautifully furnished rooms, with wide, polished floorboards, beamed ceilings and lattice-work balconies and cupboards, is ranged around an internal patio, bright with bougainvillea, and an external one shaded by a huge fig tree.

The second of Teguise's palaces, now used as a small art gallery for the works of local artists, is the **Palacio de Herrera y Rojas** (Mon–Sat 10am–1.30pm when there is an exhibition; admission fee). The third, the **Palacio del Marques**, is now a restaurant and tapas bar, the Patio del Vino *(see page 138)*, where, for the price of a drink (if you do not want a meal), you can admire the elegant dining room and large, shady patio.

A final place to visit lies just outside Teguise (take a right turn from the main road and drive up a steep but well-surfaced road). This is the **Castillo de Santa Bárbara y Museo del Emigrante** (Mon–Fri 10am–5pm, Sat–Sun 10am–4pm; admission fee), set on the top of the long-extinct Volcán de Guanapay. Built in the mid-16th century, this imposing building gave refuge to the people of Teguise and the surrounding countryside during repeated attacks by Turkish, French and English pirates. One particularly ferocious attack left the streets of Teguise running with blood, the island ransacked and the people starving. The castle is worth a visit to learn about local history and admire the far-reaching views, but the museum, devoted to Canarian emigration from the 16th to the early 20th century, is the most fascinating aspect. Documents, personal effects and early photographs tell the story of a poverty-stricken people who left for the Americas, either seeking a better life or, during a period in the 17th and 18th centuries, sent by the Spanish Crown to populate the colonies.

The Casa-Museo Palacio Spínola in Teguise

Tinajo

From Teguise a road leads northwest to **Tinajo**, about 5km (3 miles) away. The **Iglesia de San Roque** has statues by José Luján Pérez (1756–1815), the renowned Canarian sculptor. However, you must take your chance on finding it open. Near by, the village of **Mancha Blanca** is best known for the **Ermita de los Dolores**. Inside is a statue of Nuestra Señora de los Volcanes, who is credited with saving the village by halting the lava flow from a volcanic eruption in 1824. Even if the church is closed, the snowy-white exterior is very pretty. The peace of the little village is only disturbed on 15 September when a pilgrimage *(romería)* brings people from all over the island, and a craft fair, the Feria Insular de Artesanía Tradicional, is held. From here it's a very short distance to the Timanfaya National Park Visitors' Centre, but this is best saved for a separate visit to the park *(see page 52)*.

The Rocky Coast

Instead, go north to La Santa, a village on the rocky coast that has prospered because of the proximity of the **Club La Santa**. With facilities for 64 Olympic sports (as the *Guinness Book of Records* proclaims), the club has a vast stadium, an Olympic-sized pool, an artificial lake for windsurfing, and plenty of facilities for people of all abilities (or none), as well as those designed for training serious international sportspeople. If you want to visit the fishing village of **La Caleta de Famara**, the only other settlement on this coast, you must go back to Tiagua (about 12km/8 miles) and take another road north. There are a few good fish restaurants here and an excellent sandy beach, but strong winds make it unsafe for swimming.

Club La Santa

Back at the centre of the island (the Monumento del Campesino is an excellent marker), a road runs southwest through **La Geria** wine country. You could stop at the **Bodega El Grifo Museo del Vino** (daily 10.30am–6pm; admission fee includes wine-tasting; Sun free but no tasting). Set in an old bodega, the museum exhibits wine-making equipment and has a good

Vines growing on *picón* soil in La Geria wine country

display on barrel-making; and, of course, there's wine for sale. Next door to El Grifo is the **Bodega Barreto**, owned by the oldest wine-producing family on the island. There's no museum here, but you can sample and purchase their wine. Drive on through the landscape of coiled lava and vineyards, where the vines growing in the *picón* (cinders) are planted within semi-circles of volcanic rocks to stop the soil blowing away in Lanzarote's strong winds. This road will take you to Uga and the Parque Nacional de Timanfaya *(see page 52)*.

Puerto del Carmen

Lying just 5km (3 miles) west of the airport, **Puerto del Carmen** is Lanzarote's biggest resort. Its splendid beaches, Playa Grande and Playa de los Pocillos, and the less popular Playa Matagorda (closest to the airport), extend eastwards for 6km (4 miles) from the little fishing harbour that was the heart of the original village.

Until the 1970s this was just a quiet fishing community, and the area around the pretty harbour retains its village atmosphere. There is a little church here, **Nuestra Señora del Carmen**, but you will only find the doors open for mass (Sat 8.30pm, Sun 11am and 7pm). There are numerous fish restaurants, too, mostly with excellent views. You can still see fish being unloaded from small fishing smacks by the jetty, but these vessels have been joined by leisure craft and excursion boats offering trips around the coast and across to Fuerteventura. The little rocky coves just east of the harbour, before the beaches begin, are popular with divers.

The golden sands of **Playa Grande**, lined with sunbeds *(hamacas)* and bright umbrellas for rent, offer all kinds of diversions – banana boats, pedalos in the shape of giant swans, beach cafés and, of couse, glorious waters. Parallel to the beach is the **Avenida de las Playas**. Along the sea-side runs

The inviting golden sands of Puerto del Carmen

an attractive promenade, planted with palms and flowering shrubs. Here you will find the helpful little **tourist office** (Mon–Fri 10am–5pm), next door to a small gift shop belonging to the Fundación Manrique, as well as Lanzarote's only **casino**, a couple of nice restaurants, and a few little villa complexes. On the other side, the avenue resembles a vast amusement arcade, lined with cafés, bars and restaurants – mostly with Irish or English names, advertising Guinness, fish and chips and all-day English breakfasts, all at knock-down prices – along with tourist-oriented shops and kiosks offering tattos and hair-braiding. At intervals there are *centros comerciales*, with more shops and restaurants, and it is here that most of the late-night bars and clubs are found. Just past a rocky headland, the Punta de Barranquillo, these commercial outlets peter out, to be replaced with some smart little residential complexes. Then, where the **Playa de los Pocillos** commences, so do more shops and bars, but these are far more low-key than the earlier ones.

   Puerto Calero is named after the developer José Calero, who initiated the construction of the marina in 1986. It lies about 4km (2½ miles) south of Puerto del Carmen and styles itself a *puerto deportivo* – a sports port. Its smart harbour is full of sleek yachts, its restaurants full of sleek people. You can charter a boat here if you fancy a day's deep-sea fishing *(see page 82)*. If you're just dropping in for a look around, it's easiest to take a boat trip from Puerto del Carmen, so you don't have to worry about parking, which tends to be a problem.

THE SOUTH

The south of Lanzarote encompasses the extraordinary volcanic wilderness of the Parque Nacional de Timanfaya, the pretty, arty village of Yaiza, Playa Blanca, the island's southernmost resort, with its splendid beaches, and the wild jagged coast to the west.

A camel ride around the volcanic slopes

Parque Nacional de Timanfaya

Going south from the airport, take the LZ2 motorway towards Tías, from where a straight (but non-motorway) stretch continues to Yaiza (about 18km/11 miles). Just before Yaiza lies the little village of **Uga**, looking rather like a Moorish settlement, with flat-roofed white houses surrounded by palms. About 3km (2 miles) further on a bypass encircles Yaiza. From a roundabout as you approach is a narrow road leading to the **Parque Nacional de Timanfaya** (daily 9am–5.45pm, last tour 5pm; admission fee). On the way up you pass the **Echadero de Camellos** (Camel Station) where visitors are taken for rides around the outer volcanic slopes on dromedaries (single-humped camels). There's also a small museum of volcanic rocks here. The national park is one place that all visitors to Lanzarote include on their itineraries, and it's a place that few will ever forget. It is an experience that makes one aware of the awesome power of nature.

Bus tours around the **Montañas del Fuego** (Mountains of Fire) start from outside El Diablo restaurant and run throughout the day. There is a good recorded commentary in Spanish, English and German, giving background information about the park and about the volcanic eruptions that caused this once fertile area to be turned into a sea of lava. There are frequent photo stops at particularly dramatic points, but you are not allowed to get off the bus. Once the tour is over, most visitors stop to watch park attendants throwing dried brush into a hole in the ground, whereupon flames roar upwards; or pouring buckets of water into a small crater, causing a cascade of boiling water to shoot into the air.

In the glass-sided restaurant, designed, of couse, by César Manrique, you can have a drink or snack, or eat meat that has been grilled over the natural heat emanating from just below the surface (you can watch chefs officiating over the barbecue at the back of the restaurant, so you know that they are not cheating).

Visiting Timanfaya National Park

At the entrance to the park, where Manrique's famous 'fire devil' sign stands, is a barrier, where you pay an entrance fee. You will probably have to join a queue while you wait for a space to become available in the car park, from where buses take visitors on a 40-minute tour of the Ruta de los Volcanes (included in the entrance price). At busy times – late morning seems to be prime time – the wait may be as long as an hour. Take drinking water and something to amuse children when they get bored. You are not allowed to walk, or drive, through the centre of the park, but you can drive around the periphery, and drop in at the Interpretation and Visitors' Centre at the Tinajo end. Any cars you see going straight ahead instead of waiting at the barrier are doing just that.

Yaiza

The visit over, return to the roundabout and take the road straight into **Yaiza**. This village relishes its reputation as the prettiest on Lanzarote – and it certainly is very picturesque. Some typically Canarian-style buildings survived the eruption that wiped out most of the village in the 1730s, and these have been complemented by later ones in the same style. Palms line the road as you approach, scarlet geraniums decorate green balconies and bougainvillea drips over snowy-white garden walls. In the central square is the church of **Nuestra Señora de los Remedios**, which has columns of volcanic rock and a beautiful painted wooden ceiling; unlike many of the island churches, it is usually open. By contrast the **Galería Yaiza** (Mon–Sat 5–7pm; free), at the west end of the village, has good exhibitions of contemporary art, but the limited opening hours mean you'll have to make a special effort to see them.

Yaiza has several good restaurants, but is especially famous for **La Era**, set in a farmhouse dating from the early 18th century which was converted by Manrique and an architect friend, Luis Ibáñez, in the 1960s. You can have a peek inside the pretty courtyard even if you are not eating here, but why stint yourself? A meal here is a delight, but you should make a reservation, and don't turn up in beach wear.

Playa Blanca

The road from Yaiza leads south, through the bare, flat lands called El Rubicón, to **Playa Blanca**. This is Lanzarote's third resort, smaller, quieter and more upmarket than the other two. It used to be a flourishing fishing village, and retains something of that atmosphere, even as it has expanded.

The heart of the resort centres on the main street, Avenida de Papagayo, its pedestrianised extension, Calle Limones, and the Paseo Marítimo, a promenade lined with restaurants

One of Playa Blanca's appealing seaside restaurants

that runs parallel to the soft sands of **Playa Dorada** (Golden Beach) and **Playa Blanca** (White Beach) and leads to the port. West of the port, another tree-lined promenade runs round the Punta Limones headland to pretty little Playa Flamingo, backed by landscaped gardens, and with calm, safe waters. Across a narrow stretch of the Atlantic, the sands of Corralejo, on Fuerteventura, gleam in the sunlight.

Playa Blanca is big on watersports and all kinds of maritime excursions, whether you want to scuba dive, windsurf or simply take a trip in a glass-bottomed submarine *(see pages 81 and 83)*.

How long Playa Blanca will retain its fishing-village atmosphere is hard to say. Already, *urbanizaciones* stretch to the left and right (where most of the big hotels and villa complexes are situated), and on the approach to the village new buildings are going up fast. The Cabildo Insular is worried that things are getting out of hand, and in 2006 called on the district authorities to reverse some 200 planning permissions they had granted in the area, or face legal proceedings. To the east of town, new roads lead to the **Marina Rubicón**, a brand new sports marina surrounded by apartment complexes and a huge shopping and leisure centre. Not everyone is happy about this, either. On the wall of a row of neglected fishermen's cottages, where a few fish are pinned on a line to dry, and a tattered black flag flutters in the breeze, a sign in three languages reads 'There used to be a beach here'.

Further east, in a protected area known as **Los Ajaches**, lie Lanzarote's best beaches – **Playa de las Mujeres** and **Playa del Papagayo**. Don't risk driving along the dirt road that theoretically gives access to them: insurance on hired cars does not cover you for 'off-road' driving, and the emergency services will not come and get you if you run into trouble. Instead, take the Princess Yaiza Taxi Boat, which leaves four times a day from the harbour and the Marina Rubicón.

Salinas de Janubio and El Golfo

Parallel to the main road from Yaiza is another, the 701, which branches off westwards to the **Salinas de Janubio**. Salt production was one of the most important industries in

---

Particles of Peridot

The glimmers and glitters you will notice in the black-sand beach at El Golfo come from tiny particles of peridot, a semi-precious stone that is also called olivine, and ranges in colour from olive to lime-green. You will see peridot necklaces and bracelets for sale all over the island. It is the August birthstone and is believed to bring good luck. The stones used to be called evening emeralds, and it is said that the crusaders, who found them around the Red Sea, believed they *were* emeralds and brought them back home to adorn churches.

Lanzarote, but its main purpose was to preserve fish rather than for domestic use, and it is not needed in great quantities now that the catch can be refrigerated. These salt pans are the only ones still in use and they are an impressive sight, laid out like a patchwork quilt, the colour of each pan depending on the relative amount of water and salt it contains.

Los Hervideros

They are also an excellent spot for birdwatching, especially during the spring and autumn migratory periods.

A short way further up this rocky, deeply eroded coast is a spot known as **Los Hervideros** (The Boiling Pans). You will see coaches in the large car park, for this is a stopping point for tours coming from Timanfaya. It gained its name because the seething sea appears to boil in blowholes and underwater lava caves created by a volcanic tube emerging into the sea. Continue up the coast (where there are plenty of lay-bys to allow drivers to stop and admire the craggy coastline) and you soon arrive at **El Golfo**, a fishing village set between volcanic hills and pounding sea. It's just a collection of pretty cottages and fish restaurants, with outside tables by the sea. To the southern side of the village, the shell of a volcanic crater has been eroded into a jagged, richly coloured cliff. At its foot lie a small black beach and a vivid green **lagoon**, also called El Golfo. You must park at the entrance to the village and follow a footpath in order to find it.

From El Golfo the 702 leads back to Yaiza, from where you pick up the main road back towards Arrecife and the airport. Your tour of this diverse island is over.

FUERTEVENTURA

On arriving at the coast of Fuerteventura in 1402, Jean de Béthencourt was reputed to have exclaimed '¡Que aventura más fuerte!' (What a great adventure!). At least that's one theory about the origin of the island's name. Others, more prosaically, believe it derives from *viento fuerte* – strong wind. Winds are certainly a feature of the island, and one that draws surfers, windsurfers, kitesurfers and parasailors to its gorgeous sandy beaches. In the north there are the long stretches around El Cotillo and those at Corralejo, now protected in a Parque Natural. In the south, the sands stretch from Tarajalejo to Morro Jable and beyond. But there is more to the island than beaches: the sleepy little towns in the interior are the keepers of the island's history, and are places where life goes on pretty much as it has for centuries. We begin with the capital, then travel north before visiting the centre and south of the island.

THE NORTH

The north of the island is a diverse area that encompasses the capital, Puerto del Rosario; a number of inland towns and villages, set amid bare conical hills, where you can learn about cheese-making, *gofio* milling and the island's agricultural past; and the harbours, dunes and beaches of Corralejo to the east and El Cotillo in the west.

Puerto del Rosario

Puerto del Rosario lies about 7km (4 miles) north of the airport. The town was founded in 1795, called Puerto de Cabras (Goat Port), and became the island capital in 1860 (taking over the role from La Oliva). The name was changed in 1956,

Getting an overview of Fuerteventura's desert landscape

Stone fisherman on the sea wall

but the goat motif is fairly evident in statuary and in a pastoral metallic mural. A small, busy port is used by ferries from Arrecife, container ships and, more recently, cruise liners. Puerto del Rosario is not a tourist-oriented town, but is worth a brief visit. The harbour front has been renovated in recent years and is a pleasant place to walk. Palms offer shade along the inland side, and the sea wall is lined with sinuous benches decorated with coloured tiles. An area designated the Parque de Mayores is a kind of outdoor gym for elderly people, with a variety of exercise machines (well used during the cooler hours of the day) and notices warning about the dangers of over-exertion.

The town is known for its **street sculpture**, which ranges from a huge fountain on a roundabout on the Avenida Marítima, to an abstract metallic clock on another roundabout in the centre of town, to two naked dancing women in a square, and simple statues dotted all over the place – a fisherman stands on the sea wall, while an elderly man sits outside the church.

It was the church, dedicated to the **Virgen del Rosario**, that gave the town its new name. It's a simple grey-and-white building, although somewhat neglected, standing in a tree-shaded square opposite the the offices of the island government. To the side of the square is the **Casa-Museo Unamuno** (Mon–Fri 9am–2pm; free), the house (then the Hotel Fuerteventura) where the Basque writer and philosopher Miguel de Unamuno (1864–1936) lived when he was exiled here in

1924, regarded as a thorn in the flesh of Miguel Primo de Rivera's dictatorship. Unamuno's time here was brief, but he quickly came to love the country and to appreciate the kindness shown to him by the island people. They later reciprocated by erecting a huge statue of him on the lower flanks of Montaña Quemada (Burnt Mountain), just outside Tindaya. The rooms are furnished as they were in Unamuno's time, with portraits and memorabilia, and quotations from his writing about Fuerteventura are displayed on the walls.

At the roundabout where roads into Puerto del Rosario meet, you will find **Las Rotondas**, a huge new shopping centre that opened in 2006, adding greatly to the town's shopping opportunities with a range of internationally known stores.

Weaving at La Alcogida

Farms and Windmills

From Puerto del Rosario the FV10 runs northwest towards La Oliva. En route, a left turn is clearly signposted to **Tefía** and the **Ecomuseo La Alcogida** (Tues–Sun 10am–6pm; admission fee). This ingenious complex, which stretches out on either side of the road, is an abandoned farming settlement that has been restored as a museum, and allows visitors to see how rural life was lived, and what farming methods were used, during the last century. You can watch people demonstrating pulled-thread embroidery, basket-work, leather-work and weaving.

Just past the museum a road leads off to **Los Molinos** – passing, after a few hundred metres, a beautifully restored windmill, which is visible from La Alcogida. Los Molinos is a pretty little seaside village, with a couple of nice restaurants, about 8km (5 miles) west. The latter part of the road runs along the top of a gulley, the Barranco de los Molinos.

Returning to the main road and going north, you pass, on your left, **Montaña Quemada**, where Unamuno's statue blends with its craggy background; a little further on is the cheese-producing town of Tindaya and **Montaña Tindaya** (397 metres/1,303ft), which the indigenous people of the island considered a sacred mountain *(see panel)*.

La Oliva

➤ You soon come to **La Oliva**. This sleepy little town was the seat of the Guanche king, Guixe, and briefly served as the capital of the island in the early 18th century. Today, it's a workaday town, centred on a large church, **Nuestra Señora de Candelaria**, with buttressed walls and a square bell tower of volcanic stone, which makes it look as if it is

Chillida's Dream

In 1992 the Basque sculptor Eduardo Chillida put forward an ambitious proposal to create within Montaña Tindaya a vast open space. Nothing would be visible externally, but within the artist hoped to realise 'a utopia... where those who went inside would be able to see the light of the sun, the moon, to see the sea and the horizon...' The Cabildo Insular supported the plan, but there was a great deal of opposition from environmentalists. Whether or not the project would have gone ahead is unknown, as Chillida died in 2002.

Canarian Art Centre in La Oliva

growing out of the rocky landscape. The interior is plain, relatively unadorned, and the pulpit, decorated with pictures of the four Apostles, is supported on a slim, painted pedestal (put €1 in a slot by the door to gain five minutes' worth of illumination).

From the side of the Ayuntamiento, opposite the church, a straight, broad road leads to the **Casa de los Coroneles**. This grandiose and much-photographed building, with its many balconied windows, was the seat of the military rulers of the island in the early 18th century. The house is undergoing extensive restoration.

En route to the colonels' headquarters you pass the **Centro de Arte Canario** (Mon–Sat 10.30am–2pm; admission fee) in the Casa Mané, a converted colonial house. The collection of works by contemporary Canarian, or Canary Island-based, artists is somewhat eclectic, and the sculpture in the extensive cactus garden even more so, ranging from innovative abstract pieces to leaping dolphins and even some (possibly ironic) gnomes. Don't miss the galleries situated down a flight of steps and through the shop (where there are some good posters and prints for sale), as this is where some of the best work is shown, in large, light rooms.

Villaverde and Lajares

From the centre of La Oliva the FV10 leads towards the northwest coast, but it may be worth taking the slightly longer way round (up the FV101 then turning onto the FV109), because you could then stop at **Villaverde**, where the **Cueva del Llano** (Tues–Sat 10.15am–12.30pm, 2.45–5.15pm; admission fee) was first opened to the public in 2006. This *jameo*, or lava tube, was discovered in 1979, and a new species of spider, *Arácnido triglobio,* was found to be living here. A visitors' centre offers information about the

La Rosita, for a glimpse of traditional rural life

jameo, which was formed by a lava stream from nearby Montaña Escanfraga. A few kilometres north you could also visit **La Rosita** (Mon–Sat 10am–6pm; admission fee), a farm that demonstrates traditional agricultural methods, including the use of camels on the land. Children especially enjoy contact with the farm animals.

Just before the FV109 joins the FV10 to El Cotillo, you reach **Lajares**, a village with a pair of well-restored windmills on the southern outskirts, and a stadium where *lucha canaria (see page 80)* is performed. In the main street is the **Escuela de Artesanía** (Tues–Sat 10am–1pm, 5–8pm, Mon 5–8pm; free). Although called a school, it is now really more of a shop, where you can buy handmade products (not cheap) and watch local women embroidering tablecloths and napkins.

El Cotillo

The road continues about 8km (5 miles) to **El Cotillo**. Although you are greeted, on the outskirts, with a shop proclaiming that it sells 'best British products', closely followed by a fish-and-chip shop, do not be deterred. This village has a gloriously pretty little fishing harbour and a selection of good fish restaurants to go with it, plus beautiful, windswept dunes and beaches to both north and south. Beside the harbour is the **Castillo de Tostón**, a sturdy stone fortress that houses a tourist information point (Mon–Sat 9am–3pm) and a small gallery (same hours) with frequently changing exhibitions of work by local artists. El Cotillo has a small but vibrant artistic community, with some French connections. From the roof of the fort you get wonderful views down the coast. To the north, a narrow road runs through the dunes to the **Punta de Tostón**, where a lighthouse stands on an exposed headland. Quite a lot of construction work is going on in El Cotillo, and it is to be hoped that the character of the village will not be spoiled by overdevelopment.

Corralejo

Return to the main FV101 and after about 6km (4 miles) you reach **Corralejo**. (You may, of course, have started here, having come, as many do, by boat from Playa Blanca in Lanzarote; *see page 115*). Corralejo is another tiny fishing village that has expanded to cope with the demand for tourist accommodation. The heart of the town, the area around the harbour, still has a character of its own. On **Muelle Chico** (Small Jetty) there's a **tourist information kiosk** (Mon–Fri 8am–3pm, Sat–Sun 9am–3pm) close to a bronze statue called the **Monumento Marinero**, showing a returned seaman embracing his wife and child; near by, another woman looks out to sea, waiting for her husband's return. The narrow lanes that radiate from the harbour and the broad main street, Nuestra Señora del Carmen, filled with cafés, bars and shops, are reminiscent of an English seaside resort, and not just because most of the voices you hear are English. There's also something of a hippy-ish, beachcomber feel here, generated by the people who come in search of good waves and a laid-back lifestyle.

In Corralejo you can go diving and scuba diving, take a beach-buggy trip through the dunes to El Cotillo, hire a mountain bike, go on a dolphin-watching boat ride or, most popular of all, take a trip to **Isla de los Lobos** (Island of Wolves). The wolves in question were the sea lions that flourished here before they were devoured by Norman sailors who came to the island with Gadifer de la Salle's invasion force. It's a peaceful, pretty place, uninhabited, although you'll have to share it with lots of other visitors, and it's small enough to walk around in about three hours. You can see seabirds – Cory's sheerwaters nest here – and a variety of vegetation in spring and early summer. The waters are sheltered and safe even for children to swim, so it is well worth bringing a picnic and spending a day here.

The Dunes

Drive out of town on the FV1, which runs parallel to the coast through great swathes of **El Jable dunes** that are now protected as the **Parque Natural de Corralejo**. Look out for goats, which sometimes wander in the road – perhaps hoping there is something more interesting than scrubby plants to eat on the other side. On the edge of, but just inside, the park looms the huge Riu Palace Tres Islas Hotel, built before strict planning controls made such construction illegal. Thereafter, there's little but sand and more sand, low brown hills to the right, and a gorgeous sweep of turquoise waters to your left, crashing against the 10km (6 miles) of beach that draw watersports enthusiasts to this windswept area.

The road runs some 35km (22 miles) back to Puerto del Rosario, from where you can begin a tour of the centre and south of the island.

The sandy expanse of El Jable dunes

Antigua's windmill

THE CENTRE

Visiting the central part of the island offers the contrast of starting out on the coast at Caleta de Fuste, a smart, purpose-built holiday resort, then heading inland to Fuerteventura's first capital, Betancuria, and a number of other pretty towns and villages, set amid stunning mountain scenery and the occasional fertile valley.

Caleta de Fuste
Some 7km (4 miles) south of Puerto del Rosario and 9km (6 miles) south of the airport, on the FV2, lies **Caleta de Fuste**. This is a completely made-to-measure resort, clustered around a marina and the Castillo de Fuste, the 18th-century fortress from which it takes its name, and spreading inland and along the coast. Opinions are divided on Caleta de Fuste: on the one hand, it has the artificial feel of a resort created from scratch; on the other, it has been well designed, and there's a range of accommodation, good restaurants, and watersports and activities of all kinds, as well as a pleasant sandy beach. The Barceló Club El Castillo, in a prime site right by the beach, is a well-landscaped complex of attractive bungalows that resembles an entire village. To the north, a broad promenade leads along the rocky shore to Costa de Antigua; to the south, construction is going on apace up to and around the

garish new Centro Atlántico, opposite which stands Fuerteventura's only McDonald's.

Follow the road a short way south to **Las Salinas** to visit the **Museo de la Sal** (Salt Museum; Tues–Fri and Sun 9.30am–5.30pm) and the surrounding salt pans, the **Salinas del Carmen**, and learn about the extraction of salt.

Antigua

The road turns inland from here, and after about 10km (6 miles) the FV50 leads off to **Antigua**, set in the very middle of the island. Antigua used to be an important commercial centre and was briefly the capital of Fuerteventura (1834–5). Today it's a quiet town, centred on its sturdy church, **Nuestra Señora de Antigua**, one of the oldest on the island. It stands in a huge paved square, to one side of which a smaller grassy area, the **Plaza de los Caídos**, features a large cross, commemorating those who died in the Civil War. The church has a wooden ceiling and a wide nave, and is largely unadorned apart from a brightly painted main altar.

On the town's northern outskirts is the **Molino de Antigua Centro de Artesanía** (Tues–Sat 10am–6pm; admission fee). This is a fascinating complex of buildings, set in pleasant gardens. There's a windmill, where you can see the machinery used to grind *gofio*, an archeological museum and an excellent collection of craft work. The old granary has been turned into a café and restaurant that opens even on the days the museum is shut, and serves typical Canarian dishes (*see page 141*).

Just past Antigua the FV416 goes off to the left towards Betancuria. En route, if you want a stunning view over the khaki-coloured landscape and undulating hills, stop at the Mirador Morro Velosa, where there is a recently restored restaurant and viewing area, designed by César Manrique.

Betancuria

➤ **Betancuria** is a little jewel of a town, with scarcely a corner that is not picturesque, and it is well aware of its prettiness and its historical importance. 'Six hundred years of history' announces a sign on the wall of the **Ayuntamiento** (town hall) – itself a delightful building with a courtyard you can pop into. This was Fuerteventura's first capital, founded in the early 15th century by Jean de Béthencourt when his original stronghold on the coast proved not strong enough to deter pirate attacks. You can still see the remains of the Franciscan Convento de San Buenaventura, which was established here so that the brothers who followed in the conqueror's wake could bring Christianity to the native people.

There are car parks at either end of the town, which you should use – you cannot drive into the village itself,

Iglesia de Santa María

although there is some roadside parking in the main street. Here you will find the **Museo Arqueológico** (Tues–Sat 10am–5pm, Sun 11am–2pm; admission fee), with displays ranging from bones and fossils to Majorero ceramics and information on the first colonisers.

Walk through the cobbled streets to the lovely **Iglesia de Santa María** (Mon–Fri 11am–5pm, Sat 11am–3pm; small admis-

Museo de Artesanía

sion fee), consecrated in 1426, destroyed by pirates in 1593 and rebuilt a century later. Entrance to the church and the Museo de Arte Sacra usually alternates every half-hour, but the museum is currently closed and its contents are displayed in the church. The church has an intricately carved door, a splendid wooden ceiling and unusual floors – large square stones outlined with wooden boards. The ceiling in the sacristy is of *mudéjar* design, but decorated with a renaissance painting. There are some real treasures here, including a lovely retable of La Inmaculada to the left of the high altar and numerous polychromatic wooden figures of saints, some of them salvaged from the convent. The oldest part of the church, the baptistery, has a Gothic ribbed vault.

Across the square from the church, attached to the Casa de Santa María restaurant, is the **Museo de Artesanía** (Mon–Sat 11am–4pm; admission fee), arranged around a series of flower-filled courtyards. There are lots of domestic and agricultural implements, women in traditional costume demonstrating weaving, and local produce for sale at reasonable prices. Sometimes there are wine- and cheese-tastings included. Upstairs, you can watch a short film about the island.

La Vega del Río de las Palmas and Pájara

You drop down now to the 'Valley of Palms', a surprisingly green and fertile region of this dry island, where the village of **La Vega del Río de las Palmas** hosts a festival to the Virgen de la Pena (Virgin of Sorrows), patron saint of the island, on 14 June. The rest of the year it's a very sleepy place, but it has an attractive sandstone **church** (Tues–Sun 11am–1pm, 4–7pm) dedicated to the Virgin. In the same square, which is lined with art deco-style wrought-iron benches, is an excellent restaurant, **Don Antonio** *(see page 141)*.

La Vega del Río de las Palmas

The road twists and turns on its way south, but it is well surfaced, and there's a protective barrier, and lots of lay-bys where you can stop to drink in the splendid views, take photographs, or just let an impatient driver pass you by.

When the road straightens out, you come to the pretty village of **Pájara**. Palms and oleanders line the main street leading to

A detail from the doorway of Nuestra Señora de la Regla

the church of **Nuestra Señora de la Regla** (daily 11am– 1pm, 5–7pm), famous for its red sandstone doorway, carved with symbols that apear to be Aztec-influenced, including a figure with a plumed feather headdress. The church has two naves, each with a baroque high altar – put €1 in the box by the door to illuminate them.

Outside the church is a water pump with a long wooden 'arm' to which a camel used to be attached to do the heavy work of pulling up the water. To the side of the church, an at- tractive park, bright with bougainvillea in summer, lines a dry river bed. Leaving the village to the southeast, you pass a roundabout with a large sandstone statue depicting a farmer milking a goat.

Heading south now, the road rejoins the FV20 which will take you back to the capital or south to the beaches. Even if going south, you could, if you are interested in windmills, make a slight detour to **Tiscamanita** where the **Centro de Interpretación Los Molinos** (Tues–Fri and Sun 10am–5.30pm; admission fee) demonstrates the histo- ry of milling.

THE SOUTH

It is the beauty of the southern beaches, and the activities they offer, that bring most visitors to Fuerteventura. The combination of barren, elephant-coloured hills, jagged cliffs and great sweeps of white sand is irresistible, and the reliably strong winds promise windsurf enthusiasts, in particular, the time of their lives. There are also some sheltered coves, though, ideal for those who simply want to enjoy the almost perpetual sunshine. The Sotavento (Leeward) beaches on the east side of the Jandía Peninsula are the most popular; the Barlovento (Windward) beaches on the other side are only for the most hardy and experienced windsurfers. These, and the far tip of the peninsula, Punta de Jandía, are accessible only on tracks that most car-hire companies' insurance will not cover.

Gran Tarajal and Tarajalejo

Gran Tarajal, reached by a straight stretch of road off the FV2, is the island's second-largest port, and therefore has a character of its own that has not been subsumed by the tourist resort that has grown up around it. Narrow streets (where it's very hard to park) lead away from a black-sand beach and a broad promenade, planted with palms and lined with restaurants. The town hosts the Open International Fishing Competition in September each year.

From **Tarajalejo**, a little further down the coast, the main road parallels the shore. Tarajalejo is a fishing village that has developed into a resort but, although expanding rapidly, it's still low-key and pleasant. It has a 1-km (½-mile) pebbly beach and a large main square. The village is popular with sailing enthusiasts and caters well for beginners.

About 5km (3 miles) down the coast, just before the Barranco de Tarajal, lies **La Lajita**, a nice little village with a harbour. On the main road you will find **La Lajita Oasis**

Park (daily 9am–6pm; admission fee) with camel rides, giraffes, reptiles, sea lions, parrots and birds of prey, as well as an impressive botanical garden.

Playas de Sotavento

A little further down the coast a secondary road leads 5km (3 miles) across the narrow neck of the peninsula to the village and beach of **La Pared** (don't ever windsurf here alone – the currents are very dangerous). A wall *(pared)*, built by the indigenous Majoreros, stretched across here when the first conquerors arrived, and now it roughly forms the boundary of the **Parque Natural de Jandía**, which reaches down to the tip of the peninsula, measuring some 14,320 hectares (35,385 acres).

Next, you come to **Costa Calma** and the start of the long white beaches of Sotavento. Development at Costa Calma began in the 1970s and has expanded ever since, encompassing

One of the idyllic beaches of Costa Calma

a variety of accommodation, most of it block-booked by German tour companies, with the hotels providing most of the restaurants and entertainment their guests need.

A little further south, on the beautiful **Playa Barca**, the huge Hotel Los Gorriones commands a prime position. It is here that the world's largest windsurfing centre, the Pro Center René Egli, is located, and where the PWA/ISA Windsurfing and the PKRA Kiteboarding World Championships are held in late July–early August. You don't have to be a champion to windsurf here, but you do have to be careful.

Continuing down this overdeveloped coast, you will come to **Playa de Matorral** (confusingly also known as Playa de Jandía), where the long white beach has been subject to a rash of huge hotels, apartment blocks, shops and restaurants. A section of the Matorral area has now been designated a Site of Special Scientific Interest, in an attempt to preserve the vegetation and varied bird life of its salt marshes, and an EU project has been launched to raise awareness of the damage that is being done by uncontrolled development. On the **Punta de Matorral** stands a lighthouse, with a little café at its feet.

Morro del Jable

Playa de Matorral merges with **Morro del Jable**, the southernmost resort on the peninsula – after this the concrete developments thin out. Morro del Jable is a proper town with a proper port, even though hotels and apartment blocks have stretched their tentacles up the hillsides behind it. There's an

From Morro del Jable Naviera Armas ferries run to Las Palmas de Gran Canaria seven times a week, taking about 2½–3 hours.

attractive seaside promenade, some good fish restaurants and opportunities for all kinds of watersports.

The North of the Peninsula

The roads beyond Morro del Jable down to Puerto de la Cruz and the Punta de Jandía, and round to Cofete on the northern side of the peninsula, are not to be recommended unless you have a four-wheel-drive vehicle, and even then you should check the details of your insurance cover. There is no road going across the peninsula, just a ridge of mountains cut through with *barrancos* (gullies) and dominated by **Montaña de Jandía**, the highest peak on the island at 807 metres (2,648ft). The most common form of vegetation here is the *cardón de Jandía (Euphorbia handiensis)*, the symbol of Fuerteventura, and in the most inaccessible regions the *tajinaste de Jandía (Echium handiense)*. The beaches at the peninsula's tip and the **Playa de Cofete** and **Playa de Barlovento** (both favoured by nudists) on the other side are largely deserted, undeniably beautiful, and swept by high winds. Rocks are sculpted into jagged forms, sea spurge survives on the dunes, and a few goats are the only sign of wildlife. The tiny hamlet of **Cofete** is known only for the Villa Winter, an abandoned house built by a Nazi sympathiser on land allegedly given to him by General Franco. All kinds of rumours have surrounded this villa over the years, but this untamed region is just the sort of place in which rumours flourish and myths are created.

WHAT TO DO

Most of the things you can do in Lanzarote and Fuerteventura are done outdoors, many of them on or in the
water. Ideal winds and waves make windsurfing the most
popular activity, but there are many others – sailing, diving,
fishing, swimming and lots of boat trips. On land, there are
some good hiking trails, opportunities for horse riding and
exploring the rougher terrain by jeep, buggy or quad bike
safari, and plenty of activities for children.

SPORTS AND OUTDOOR ACTIVITIES

Windsurfing

On **Lanzarote** the Windsurfing Club Nathalie Simon, Calle
de las Olas 18, Playa de las Cucharas, Costa Teguise, tel: 928
590 731, <www.sportaway-lanzarote.com>, offers advanced,
beginners' and children's courses, plus other activities *(see
page 86)*. Windsurf Paradise, Calle la Corvina 8, Playa de las
Cucharas, Costa Teguise, tel: 928 346 022, <www.windsurf
lanzarote.com>, also offers lessons, from basic to advanced
levels, and surfing trips to other beaches on the island.

On **Fuerteventura** a selection of operators includes: The
Fanatic Fun Centre, Costa Calma, tel: 928 547 214; Windsurf
El Castillo, Caleta de Fustes, tel: 928 163 100; Ventura Surf
Center, Apartamentos Hoplaco, Correlejo, tel: 928 866 295,
<www.ventura-surf.com>; and the Pro Center René Egli I,
Hotel Los Gorriones, Playa la Barca, tel: 928 547 025,
<www.rene-egli.com>, which is *the* name in windsurfing.
There is a second centre, René Egli II, about 3km (2 miles)
further south, where winds are not as quite as strong.

Windsurfing is popular on both islands

Kitesurfing

Kitesurfing attracts enthusiasts to **Fuerteventura**. Try the Kiteboarding School of Fuerteventura, El Cotillo, tel: 928 538 504, <www.ksfuerte.com>, and Flag Beach Windsurf and Kitesurf Centre, <www.flagbeach.com>, in Corralejo.

Surfing

Lanzarote surf schools include Calima Surf, Caleta de Famara, tel: 928 528 528, mobile: 626 913 369, <www.calimasurf.com>, which offers 'theory and practice' lessons; Famara Surf, Avda El Marinero 39, Caleta de Famara, tel/fax: 928 528 676, <www.famarasurf.com>, for classes at all levels and equipment for hire or sale; the Quiksilver Surf School, tel: 928 867 307, www.quiksilver-surfschool.com, for surfing (with or without accommodation packages) in Lanzarote and Fuerteventura; and Windsurf Paradise (see page 79 for details).

There is less surfing in **Fuerteventura**, but Ineika Funcenter, Corralejo, tel/fax: 928 535 744, <www.ineika.com>,

---

Lucha Canaria

Lucha canaria is a popular sport that dates back to pre-Hispanic times. It is a form of wrestling in which members of two teams of 12 wrestlers take it in turns to throw an opponent to the ground. The bout *(brega)* is lost if any part of a wrestler's body (except his feet, of course) touches the ground. You are most likely to see the sport at village fiestas, and there is a demonstration in Teguise on Sunday market day, around noon. It also takes up hours of Saturday-night prime-time television on the regional channel, and generates strong feelings. Another traditional local sport is *juego del palo*, or stick-fighting. The object is to keep the body as still as possible, while fending off the blows from an opponent's stave – a stick about 1.8 metres (6ft) long. Again, you are most likely to see one of these bouts at a village festival; ask at a local tourist office.

caters for beginners and advanced surfers, and arranages transfers to the best surf spots on the island.

Diving

For diving in **Lanzarote**'s three main resorts, contact Calipso Diving, Pueblo Marinero, Costa Teguise, tel: 928 590 879, <www.calipso-diving.com>, which runs PADI/BSAC courses, plus fam-

Snorkelling in clear waters

ily snorkelling excursions; Lanzarote Dive Service, Hotel de las Arenas, Playa de los Charcos, mobile: 616 215 734, <www.lanzarotedive.de>, for children's courses, beginners' PADI courses and advanced courses, scuba diving and wreck and cave diving; Manta Diving, Avda Juan Carlos I 6, Local 5, Puerto del Carmen, tel: 928 516 815, mobile: 649 121 142, <www.manta-diving-lanzarote.com>, also offers PADI courses and daily dives for groups and individuals, and specialises in 'Discover Scuba' shallow-water dives and snorkelling for children. In Playa Blanca the Rubicón Diving Center, Puerto Deportivo Marina Rubicón, tel: 928 349 346, <www.rubicon diving.com>, runs courses at various levels and takes Saturday trips to Isla de los Lobos, off Fuerteventura.

Diving opportunities are also numerous on **Fuerteventura**, especially in Corralejo. Abyss Divers, Pro Centre, Corralejo, tel: 928 537 297, mobile: 638 722 297, is Irish-owned and has a good reputation. Dive Center Corralejo, Nuestra Señora del Pino 22, Corralejo, tel: 928 535 906, <www.divecentercorralejo.com>, takes divers to more than 40 sites, runs classes at all levels and has an indoor pool for scuba instruction. Punta Amanay Dive Center, Calle El Pulpo s/n, Edificio Dunas Club,

Fishing can be social or solitary

Corralejo, tel: 928 535 357, <www.punta-amanay.com>, runs dives in El Cotillo, El Jablito, Caleta de Fuestes and Morro Jable, although based in Corralejo. In Jandía, there's the Club Aldiana, Ctra de Jandía s/n, tel: 928 541 447, and the long-established Hotel Robinson Club, Playa de Matorral, tel: 928 541 375 or 928 544 033, for scuba diving and windsurfing.

Sport Fishing

The biggest operator in **Lanzarote** runs *Mizu I, Mizu II* and *Mizu III* from Puerto Calero marina, mobile: 636 474 000, <www. sportfishinglanzarote.com>, offering shark fishing, bottom fishing and trawling on well-equipped boats. Transport to and from your hotel and lunch are included in all-day trips. It also does private charters, and operates on **Fuerteventura**. Also on Fuerteventura, there's *Barvik* on Corralejo's Muelle Deportivo, tel: 928 535 710, and *Pez Velero*, tel: 928 866 173.

Sailing

In **Lanzarote**, Active Adventures, based in Costa Teguise, offers sailing among its other activities, UK tel: 0845 838 5953, <www.activeadventures.co.uk>. In Puerto Calero, you can have a two-day introductory sailing course, <www.yacht aholic.com>. Sailing schools offer catamaran lessons on Top

Cat catamarans in Tarajalejo and Las Playitas, **Fuerteventura**. They claim an absolute beginner can learn to sail a catamaran in around 12 hours, <www.learn-catamaran-sailing.com>.

Boat Trips

Among many companies competing for business in **Lanzarote** are *Ana Segundo* Express Water Bus, tel: 928 514 322, with hourly departures every day in summer from Puerto del Carmen harbour to Puerto Calero marina; Líneas Marítimas Romero, Calle García Escámez 11, Isla Graciosa, tel: 902 401 666 or 928 842 055, <www.lineas-romero.com>, with trips from Órzola to Isla Graciosa five times a day in high summer; and Papagayo Sailing, Playa Blanca harbour, mobile: 610 693 644, <www.lanzarote.com/alex>, where you can hire a yacht and its captain, Alex, for one-, four- or six-hour trips.

Princesa Ico, Puerto del Carmen, tel: 928 514 322, is a glass-bottomed catamaran that makes 'dolphin search' trips, and day trips and straightforward crossings to Corralejo. It will pick up from hotels. *Princess Yaiza*, Playa Blanca, tel: 928 514 322, is a glass-bottomed boat that makes trips from Playa Blanca harbour and Marina Rubicón to Playa de Papagayo four times a day.

Rubicat, Marina Rubicón, Playa Blanca, tel: 928 519 012, operates from the new marina to Playa Papagayo, with opportunities for jet-skiing and snorkelling. Submarine Safaris, Módulo C, Puerto Calero, tel: 928 512 898, <www.submarinesafaris.com>, makes trips beneath the sea in a yellow (naturally) submarine.

The yellow submarine

A jeep safari kicking up dust

Most of **Fuerteventura**'s boat trips tend to be in the north of the island, where the winds and waves are not as strong as in the south. Catlanza, Puerto de Corralejo, mobile: 647 061 991, <www.catlanza.com>, organises catamaran trips to Isla de los Lobos, with snorkelling, lunch and jet-ski ride included (also trips from Puerto Calero, Lanzarote, to Corralejo, tel: 928 513 022); Excursiones Marítimas, Puerto de Corralejo (buy tickets at the harbour kiosk) run three trips a day to Isla de los Lobos, no frills, and much cheaper than the alternatives. In the south, Subcat, Avda de Saladar 1, Jandía, tel: 928 166 392, <www.subcat-fuerteventura.com>, Fuerteventura's only submarine, takes you 30 metres (100ft) below the surface.

Jeep and Quad Bike Safaris

In **Lanzarote**'s resorts there is Quad Safari Lanzarote, mobile: 639 227 227 (free pick-up from Puerto del Carmen and Costa Teguise) for bike and buggy excursions; MegaFun

Lanzarote, Centro Comercial Costa Mar, Playa de los Pocillos, Puerto del Carmen, tel: 928 512 893, <www.megafunlanzarote.com>, for three-hour quad bike excursions; and Tamarán Jeep Safari, tel: 928 512 475, <www.tamaran.com>, offering extensive tours of the island from Tahiche to Playa Blanca; it will pick up from the resorts.

In **Fuerteventura** Buggy Tour, Parque Holandés, Bella Vista 7, Corralejo, tel: 928 539 074 or mobile: 618 525 258, has twin-seater buggies to make the Corralejo–El Cotillo round trip; Fuerteventura BugX Desert Tours, Corralejo, tel: 928 535 185 or mobile: 607 933 764, run a 40km (24-mile) quad buggy tour through the Corralejo–El Cotillo desert landscape.

Bike Hire and Tours

On **Lanzarote** try Bike Station, Centro Comercial Las Maretas, Avda Isla de las Canarias, Costa Teguise, mobile: 628 102 177; Papagayo Sport Center, Playa Blanca, mobile: 606 109 765, which will deliver and collect bikes from your accommodation; and Renner Bike, Avda de las Playas, Centro Comercial Marítimo 25, Puerto del Carmen, tel/fax: 928 510 612, <www.mountainbike-lanzarote.com>. **Fuerteventura** has BikeCenter, Suite Hotel Atlanta Fuerteventura Resort, Calle Las Dunas s/n, Corralejo, tel: 928 535 362, <www.mp-sports.de>, for bike hire and excursions of varying levels; Backtrax at Hotel Elba Antigua Suites, Caleta de Fustes, tel: 928 160 206, does off-road motorbike tours; Rent A Bike, Avda Juan Carlos I, Corralejo, tel: 928 866 233, hires bikes and scooters; and Ventura Biking, Calle Gran Canaria 2 Corralejo, mobile: 637 40 82 33, <www.ventura-biking.com>, offers mountain-bike tours.

> **Bike and buggy hire and excursions include insurance (check whether it is third-party or comprehensive) and provide helmets, but you need a driving licence and a credit card as a deposit.**

Hiking

On **Lanzarote** Canary Trekking, Calle La Laguna 8, Costa Teguise, mobile: 609 537 684, fax: 928 826 114, <www.canarytrekking.com>, conducts guided walks in Timanfaya National Park, the Playa de Famara Natural Park, and the protected landscape of La Geria. Windsurfing Club Nathalie Simon *(see page 79)* also offers guided walks through volcanic landscapes. On **Fuerteventura** Caminata, Villa Volcana, Villaverde, tel: 928 535 010, organises a variety of treks.

Horse and Camel Riding

Lanzarote a Caballo, Crta Arrecife–Yaiza, Km 17, Yaiza, tel: 928 830 038, <www.lanzaroteacaballo.com>, offers treks of varying lengths for beginners and experienced riders. Camel rides are also available.

Taking to the saddle at Lanzarote a Caballo

Golf

On **Lanzarote** Costa Teguise Golf Club, Avda del Golf s/n, Costa Teguise, tel: 928 590 512, <www.lanzarote-golf.com>, is an 18-hole course open to non-members that also offers lessons. (Golf courses are under construction outside Puerto del Carmen and Playa Blanca.) On **Fuerteventura** there's the Fuerteventura Golf Resort, Ctra de Jandía, Km 11, Caleta de Fustes, tel: 928 160 034, <www.fuerteventuragolfresort.com>.

CHILDREN'S ACTIVITIES

There's lots for children to do on both islands, as well as play on the beach. Taking them out in the evening isn't a problem, either, as most restaurants, as in the rest of Spain, welcome children. Many hotel complexes have evening entertainment geared to children between three and ten years old. Most children, except the very young ones, will also enjoy the boat and submarine trips listed above and many of the activities detailed in the *Where to Go* chapter, such as the bus tour around the Ruta de Volcanos.

Water Parks

There is one on each island. On **Lanzarote** it is Aquapark, Avda de Teguise, Costa Teguise, tel: 928 592 128, with all the usual pools, chutes, slides and activities to suit kids of all ages (daily 10am–6pm). On **Fuerteventura** there is Baku Park, Corralejo, <www.bakufuerteventura.com> (daily mid-June–mid-Sept 10am–6pm; mid-Sept–Nov, Mar–May 10am–5pm), for all kinds of watery fun in a well-laid-out park.

Go-Karting

Go-Karting Club, Ctra Arrecife–Tías Km 7 (2km/1 mile from **Lanzarote** airport), mobile: 619 759 946, <www.grankarting.com> (daily 11am–9pm), offers tracks for children aged 16 and under, and 'senior tracks' for the parents; five-year-olds can learn on their own special track.

Animal Attractions

One of **Lanzarote**'s best-known attractions is Echadero de Camelos, Parque Nacional de Timanfaya (daily 9am–5.45pm), where children and adults alike find it hard to resist the fun of riding the camels. Lanzarote a Caballo (daily 10am–6pm; *see page 86*) is a good riding school for adults and children; they also do paintball sessions. Las Pardelas, Órzola, tel: 928 842 545 (daily 10am–6pm) is a family-run place with donkey rides and a children's playground. At Parque Tropical, Guinate (5km/3 miles north of Haría), tel: 928 835 500 (daily 10am–5pm), exotic birds, monkeys and meerkats are the highlights for children. Rancho Texas, Puerto del Carmen, tel: 928 841 286, <www.ranchotexaslanzarote.com>, puts on shows several times a day; there are crocodiles, parrots and birds of prey, plus canoes and pony rides (daily 9.30am–5.30pm; free transport from hotels in all resorts).

The reptile show at Fuerteventura's La Lajita Oasis Park

One of **Fuerteventura**'s big draws is Oceanarium Explorer, Puerto Castillo Yacht Harbour, Caleta de Fuste, tel: 928 163 514, with a 'touch tank' aquarium, a glass-bottomed submarine and a chance to swim with sea lions. Also popular is La Lajita Oasis Park, Ctra General de Jandía s/n, La Lajita, tel: 902 400 434 (daily 9am–6pm), with camel rides, giraffes, reptiles, sea lions, parrots and birds of prey. At Zoo Safari, Ctra Majanicho, Lajares, tel: 928 868 006 (Mon–Sat 10am–5pm), there are camel safaris and a chance to explore the crater of Calderón Hondo (must be pre-booked) for older children and adults, as well as shorter camel rides closer to the litttle camel farm.

SHOPPING

Shopping is not a major activity on either island, but there are some interesting items. Among them are consumables: *mojo* sauce can be bought in small jars in many places, as can cactus honey, wine from La Geria and the ubiquitous rum-and-honey liqueur called Ronmiel. Majorero cheese, made in Fuerteventura, can also be bought on both islands.

Aloe vera products of all kinds can be found everywhere, at reasonable prices. There are some specialist shops and stalls in markets, but products are also available in souvenir shops and supermarkets. Lanzaloe is an ecologically aware organisation based in Órzola that supplies large quantities of aloe vera to pharmaceutical and cosmetics companies. Other things you will see on sale include ceramics – nothing startlingly original, but you can find some good modern copies of traditional pottery – and peridot jewellery *(see page 56)*. There is also hand-embroidered table linen, basket work and traditional-style hats made of palm leaves. The genuine articles are usually found in artisans' centres or museums and, because it is such labour-intensive work, are quite expensive.

Some places in **Lanzarote** worth checking out for comestibles are: Ahumaderia Uga, Ctra Arrecife–Yaiza, Uga, for excellent smoked salmon; El Gourmet Deli, Calle Canalejas 8, Arrecife, which has a good selection of delicatessen items – cheese, ham, *mojo* sauces and honey as well as local wine; and the Bodega El Grifo and Bodega Barreto, next door to each other on the main road at La Florida, which both sell their own wine. The white *malvasía* is best, whether you like it sweet, dry or medium. You can taste before you buy.

For craft work, there is the Centro Artesanía de Haría, Plaza de León y Castillo, Haría, a co-operative that sells pottery, basket work and embroidered items, which can also be found in Haría's Saturday market. The Centro de Artesanía at the Monumento del Campesino, Mozaga, sells traditional-stye items made on the premises, as well as wine from nearby La Geria.

Traditional-style ceramics

The Fundación César Manrique in Tahiche has a good selection of items with the artist's designs, ranging from prints and ceramics to canvas bags, scarves and aprons – all very well-priced. The Fundación also has outlets in Teguise and in Puerto del Carmen (next to the tourist office).

Teguise market is the best-known and biggest on Lanzarote, but most of the goods are not local – a lot of them are made in the Far East. However, there are a number of shops in the town that are open on Sunday and sell better-quality stuff. These include: Casa Atrium in Calle Cruz, which stocks some attractive casual clothes and some prints; Casa Kaos, Calle León y Castillo, with a good selection of jewellery and pottery; and Galeria La Villa, Plaza Clavijo, a collection of shops selling ceramics, bags and scarves, plus a 'wellness centre' and massage services. Herbolaria Demeter, Calle León y Castillo, specialises in aloe vera products, health food and

Teguise market

candles; and the friendly Frutería La Villa, Calle José Antonio, is one of the few places that specialises in organic produce.

Majorero cheese is one of the best buys in **Fuerteventura**. It can be found everywhere, but Hijos de Vera Montelongo, Calle de la Casa Alta 15, Tindaya, is one of the island's best-known cheese makers, and sells direct from its production centre. La Casa de Ganadero, Calle Salamanca 12, Puerto del Rosario, is an outlet of the Hijos de Vera Montelongo company.

Craftwork on Fuerteventura can be found in the Casa Santa María Centro de Artesanía, Betancuria. Traditional woven and embroidered items and pottery are sold in the museum shop, along with *mojo* sauce, cactus honey, wine and liqueurs. At the Escuela de Artesanía Canaria, Plaza Santa María, Lajares, you can see women embroidering table linen by hand and buy the products, along with souvenirs and gifts.

The best range of contemporary posters, prints and ceramics can be found in the shop at the Centro de Arte Canario, Casa Mane, La Oliva, and they are very reasonably priced.

NIGHTLIFE AND FESTIVALS

Most of the the islands' nightlife is provided either in the resort hotels, which usually have middle-of-the-road live acts several times a week, or in the bars and discos of the commercial centres, which tend to have quite a high turnover rate. Temporary structures are often set up on or near the beaches for performances by rock and pop groups. Corralejo and El Cotillo, on Fuerteventura, have the best reputation for rock, pop and jazz – posters and flyers in the resorts will tell you what's on where. El Almacén, Calle Betancort, Arrecife, sometimes has jazz, rock or guitar music (the Cabildo puts out a monthly leaflet, called *Cultura*, listing events here and in the theatres in San Bartolomé and Teguise). The centre also has a small cinema which shows art-house films, but these are all in Spanish, as are those shown in Arrecife's mainstream cinema (Charco de San Ginés).

The Heineken Jazz Festival, which attracts international performers, is held in Teguise at the end of June. In October, the Visual Music Festival of Lanzarote stages performances of contemporary music in interesting venues all over the island – the Cueva de los Verdes, the Jameos del Agua (when renovation work is completed) and the Convento de Santo Domingo in Teguise, for example.

Making music in Corralejo

There is one casino, Gran Casino de Lanzarote, Avda de las Playas 12, Puerto del Carmen, tel: 928 515 000 (5pm–4am; restaurant 7pm–3am; dress smartly and take your passport).

Calendar of Events

6 January Cabalgata de Reyes (Procession of the Three Kings), Arrecife. The kings parade through the streets on camels, throwing sweets to children. Some processions in other towns on both islands.

February–early March Carnival. Celebrations, held in most towns and resorts on both islands, are staggered so that they do not clash with each other. Several days of flamboyant fun usually start with the *murgas*, a parade of costumed revellers accompanied by whistles and drums. Carnival ends with the *entierro de la sardina*, a strange ritual common to all Spanish carnival celebrations, in which a papier-mâché model of a sardine is burnt.

Late March–mid-April Semana Santa. The week preceeding Easter is a time of solemn processions.

Mid-June Corpus Christi. Intricately designed carpets of salt, dyed various colours, cover the roads around the Iglesia de San Ginés in Arrecife, where processions are held.

23 June San Juan. On the eve of the saint's day bonfires are lit in some town and village squares. The biggest celebration is in Haría.

14 July San Buenaventura. The island's patron saint is celebrated throughout Fuerteventura but especially in Betancuria.

16 July Nuestra Señora del Carmen. The patron saint of fishermen and sailors is celebrated in most coastal places with processions in the streets and sometimes in decorated boats. The biggest celebrations on Lanzarote are in Puerto del Carmen, Playa Blanca, Isla Graciosa and, although it is inland, Teguise. On Fuerteventura, Morro Jable and Corralejo stage the most colourful events.

25 August San Ginés celebrations, in honour of Arrecife's patron saint include processions and dancing, and last about a week.

Early September Nuestra Señora de los Volcanes. According to legend, the Virgin halted the flow of lava from a volcanic eruption in 1824 and saved the village of Mancha Blanca, Lanzarote. She is honoured with a pilgrimage, a folklore festival, an artisans' fair and bouts of *lucha canaria*.

Mid-November Kite Festival: Playa del Burro, Corralejo. Kite-flyers from all over the world come to this two-day event.

EATING OUT

Canary Islands food has much in common with that of mainland Spain, but with interesting regional differences. There are also dishes similar to those found in parts of Latin America – although whether these recipes were introduced to the New World by Canarian emigrants, or American inventions brought back by returnees, is debatable.

You will also find some restaurants where the cooking is described as *cocina vasca* (Basque), because a number of cooks from this northern region of Spain have come to work on the island or opened their own restaurants here. Their familiarity with Atlantic fish and seafood may help them feel at home. As the Basque region has a reputation for some of the best cooking in Spain, they are a welcome addition.

Where and When to Eat

When it comes to places to eat, the choices are between the fish restaurants that line the seafronts and harbours; the places serving typically Canarian food, which are found mainly in the towns and villages – although there are a few in the resorts; and the all-purpose pizza, pasta and burger joints. There are a few expensive venues, but most are very reasonably priced. You may see restaurants advertising *cocina casalinga* or *comidas caseras* – this simply means home cook-

In the resorts, you may have to bypass numerous restaurants offering burgers, chips, pasta and pizza, not to mention all-day English breakfasts, before you find ones serving genuinely Canarian – or even Spanish – food, but they do exist. And good fresh fish, simply cooked, can be found almost everywhere.

Lunch is served on Playa Blanca's marina

ing, and, while the quality may vary, it is a sign that you will be getting authentic, and inexpensive, island food. There are not many places that style themselves tapas bars, but in many middle-of-the-range and inexpensive restaurants there will be a variety of tapas on offer, and some of the portions are quite large – two or three would make a meal for most people. You will also see *raciones* (portions) advertised: these are larger than tapas, but not full meals.

Bars are generally places in which to drink, not eat, although many will serve sandwiches *(bocadillos)* or a limited range of tapas. A *piscolabis* is a bar serving a variety of little sandwiches and snacks. *(See pages 134–42 for a selection of recommended restaurants.)*

The islanders, like the people of mainland Spain, eat late. Between two and three o'clock is the time to sit down to lunch, and ten o'clock is not too late for dinner. Some restaurants may close for a few hours between lunch and dinner, but many serve food all day. Those that cater mostly to foreign visitors, aware that habits are different, will have their lunch menus out by midday and serve dinner as early as you like.

Sunday lunch is a major event, and as this continues throughout the afternoon many restaurants are closed on Sunday evening. Some also close one evening during the week, and some places will close for a month in early summer to prepare themselves for their busy season in July and August.

Fish

The waters around the islands are rich in fish, which turn up on menus in the restaurants. Along with the ubiquitous *sardinas*, fresh from the ocean, the fish most commonly seen on menus are *corvina* (a kind of sea bass), *cherne* (wreckfish or stone bass), *sama* (sea bream) and *bacalao* (salt cod). You will also find *merluza* (hake), *atún* (tuna) and seafood such as *gambas* (prawns), *pulpo* (octopus), *calamares* (squid) and *almejas* (clams).

Cheese

Fuerteventura is known for its goat's cheese, Majorero, which has been awarded a *denominación de origen controlada* (DOC) and is said to be one of the best of its kind in Spain. Goat's milk – which must be unpasteurised to make the cheese – has a high fat content and is very aromatic. The young, fresh cheese has a white rind and a crumbly texture; the matured version has a yellow rind, which may be rubbed with oil or paprika or, sometimes, *gofio*. You will find it on most menus in Fuerteventura, and quite a few on Lanzarote. You will also see cheeses from Gran Canaria: *queso de flor*, a soft cheese that is a mixture of sheep's and cow's milk curdled with the juice of flowers from the cardoon thistle; and *queso tierno de Valsequillo*, which ranges in flavour from mild to strong – the stronger it is the darker the colour.

Fish will often be served simply grilled along with salad, *mojo* sauce and *papas arrugadas (see page 98)*, but there are numerous other ways that it may appear on your table. *Sancocho canario* is a popular dish, a stew made with red grouper or sea bass, potatoes and yams, spiced up with a hot variety of *mojo* sauce. *Salpicón de pescado* is another dish you may see on menus; this is sea bass cooked, chopped and served cold with a mixture of onions, garlic, tomatoes and

Fresh fish can be found everywhere

peppers, topped with hard boiled egg and olives. A delicacy introduced from the Basque country is *calamares rellenos de bacalao* – small squid with a tasty, cod-based stuffing, sometimes served in a creamy sauce (there is a similar dish made with stuffed peppers – *pimientos*).

Paella is not a Canary Island dish, but you can still find it, along with other rice and seafood dishes such as *arroz negra* (rice with squid and squid ink, which makes it black).

Meat

If you don't like fish, don't despair – there's plenty of meat to be found. *Cabrito* (kid) and *conejo* (rabbit) are most common, but pork *(cerdo)* and chicken *(pollo)* are popular, and there are some good steaks to be had as well. Goat and rabbit are often served *al salmorejo* (with green peppers, in a herb and garlic marinade). Chorizo – the red spicy sausage found all over Spain – also crops up in a variety of guises.

Soups

Most of the world's traditional dishes originated as a way of filling stomachs with what was available and inexpensive. In the Canary Islands, this meant a whole range of substantial soups and stews. *Ropa vieja* (literally, old clothes) may not sound very appetising, but it's a tasty mixture of meat, tomatoes and chickpeas; *puchero* includes meat, pumpkin and any vegetables available; while *rancho canario*, made with chicken, chorizo, bacon, chickpeas and various herbs, is the most elaborate and, some say, the best.

Vegetarians should be aware that even such innocent-sounding dishes as watercress soup *(potaje de berros)*, a staple found on many menus, has chunks of bacon in it, and celery soup *(potaje de apio)* may contain scraps of pork.

Vegetables

The vegetables you are offered will be those that are in season, and, because the island does not produce a great variety and imports are expensive, choice may be limited. Pulses such as lentils *(lentejas)* and chickpeas *(garbanzos)* are used a lot. Canary tomatoes are delicious – although most of those you get here will have been imported from Gran Canaria – and Lanzarote onions are far sweeter than those from mainland Spain. If you like garlic, ask for *tomates aliñados*, tomato salad smothered with olive oil and garlic. *Pimientos de padrón* – small green peppers cooked whole and covered with salt – originated in Galicia and are now found everywhere. Avocados (strictly speaking a fruit, not a vegetable) are served at a perfect stage of ripeness.

Most dishes contain or are accompanied by potatoes *(papas)*. You won't go far without encountering *papas arrugadas* (wrinkled potatoes), which are served with meat and fish or by themselves as tapas. They are small potatoes – the yellow-fleshed Tenerife variety are best – cooked in their skins in salted water, then left to dry over a low heat until their skins wrinkle and a salty crust forms. It is said that this dish originated with fishermen who used to boil the potatoes in sea water.

Mojo

Papas arrugadas, and many meat dishes, are usually accompanied by *mojo rojo*, a sauce whose basic ingredients are tomatoes, peppers and paprika. A spicier version *(mojo picón)* contains hot chilli pepper as well. *Mojo verde* is a green sauce made with oil, vinegar, garlic, coriander and/or parsley, usually served with fish. The sauces arrive at the table in small bowls, so you can use as much or as little as you like. Every restaurant – and probably every home – seems to have their own version, and entire *mojo* recipe books are published.

Papas arrugadas **with peppers and** *mojo rojo*

Gofio

Made of wheat, barley or a mixture of the two, *gofio* was the staple food of the Guanches and still forms an essential part of the diet today. The cereal is toasted before being ground into flour, and then has a multiplicity of uses. It is stirred into soups and into children's milk, used to thicken sauces, and mixed with oil, salt and sugar into a kind of bread, not unlike polenta. It is also blended with fish stock to make a thick soup called *gofio escaldado*.

Fruit and Desserts

There is not enough rain to grow much fruit in Lanzarote or Fuerteventura, but products imported from mainland Spain or the other islands are usually delicious when in season. On many menus desserts are limited to ice cream *(helado)*, flan (the ubiquitous caramel custard), fresh fruit, dried fruit and nuts, and the one you see everywhere, *bienmesabe*, which translates as 'tastes good to me' – and so it does. There are numerous recipes, but basically it is a mixture of crushed almonds, lemon, sugar (lots), cinnamon and egg yolks.

Dried fruit and nuts are often found on the dessert menu

What to Drink

The breakfast drink is coffee. *Café solo* is a small, strong black, like an espresso; a *cortado*, served in a glass, is a shot of coffee with a small amount of hot milk; *café con leche* is a large milky coffee. An *Americano* is a shot of coffee with added hot water. However, espresso and cappuccino are widely understood terms.

At bodegas you can try wine from the barrel before buying

Hot chocolate is sometimes available for breakfast, but if you ask for tea you will just get a teabag in a little pot.

You are advised not to drink tap water, but *agua mineral* is available everywhere – *con gas* is sparkling, *sin gas* is still. *Zumo de naranja*, freshly squeezed orange juice, is widely available, and in some bars you can get more exotic juices.

Wine is usually drunk with meals, most of it imported from the mainland; Rioja is one of the favourites. But Lanzarote does produce its own wine: *malvasía*, known in English as malmsey. Shakespeare alluded to malmsey several times, and the Duke of Clarence drowned in a vat of it in 1478. Although this is best known as a sweet wine, there are excellent dry and semi-dry varieties, and some reds, although the whites are better. The grapes are grown in the volcanic soil of the La Geria region, where you can visit bodegas, and in the far north of the island, near the Mirador del Río. El Grifo is regarded as the best, but Barreto is also a reputable producer.

You will find local wines in many restaurants, usually quite reasonably priced. Neighbouring Gran Canaria has some 32 wineries, and a recently introduced *denominación de origen controlada* (DOC); Monte Lentiscal, which has its own DOC, is one to look out for. Tenerife is a bigger producer, but its wines are not regularly found in restaurants.

Rum, some of which is produced at Arucas, Gran Canaria, forms the basis of Ronmiel, in which the spirit is blended with honey and lemon in a pleasant, sweet liqueur. You may also find Guindilla, a cherry liqueur from Gran Canaria, and Manzana Verde, an apple-based schnapps that is actually made in Cataluña but is widely available here.

Beer is extremely popular on the island. You will see familiar Spanish brands such as San Miguel, and imported German and English beers, along with the Canary Islands' own Tropical and Dorada. If you want a draught beer, ask for a *caña*.

Restaurants with terraces by the sea are always popular

To Help You Order...

Could we have a table?	¿Nos puede dar una mesa?
Do you have a set menu?	¿Tiene un menú del día?
I'd like…	Quisiera…

beer	**una cerveza**	milk	**leche**
bread	**pan**	mineral water	**agua mineral**
coffee	**un café**	potatoes	**patatas/papas**
dessert	**un postre**	rice	**arroz**
fish	**pescado**	salad	**una ensalada**
fruit	**fruta**	sandwich	**un bocadillo**
glass	**un vaso**	sugar	**azúcar**
ice cream	**un helado**	tea	**un té**
meat	**carne**	water (iced)	**agua (fresca)**
menu	**la carta**	wine	**vino**

...and Read the Menu

aceitunas	olives	**langosta**	spiny lobster
albóndigas	meatballs	**langostino**	large prawn
almejas	baby clams	**mariscos**	shellfish
anchoas	anchovies	**mejillones**	mussels
atún	tuna	**melocotón**	peach
bacalao	cod	**merluza**	hake
besugo	sea bream	**navajas**	razor clams
boquerones	fresh anchovies	**ostras**	oysters
calamares	squid	**pastel**	cake
caracoles	snails	**pollo**	chicken
cerdo	pork	**pulpitos**	baby octopus
chuletas	chops	**salsa**	sauce
cocido	stew	**sepia**	cuttlefish
cordero	lamb	**ternera**	veal
entremeses	hors-d'oeuvres	**tortilla**	omelette
gambas	prawns	**trucha**	trout
habas	broad beans	**uvas**	grapes

HANDY TRAVEL TIPS

An A–Z Summary of Practical Information

A

ACCOMMODATION *(Alojamiento)*

Most accommodation on Lanzarote is concentrated in the three major resorts: Puerto del Carmen, Costa Teguise and Playa Blanca. Self-catering apartments are far more common that hotel rooms, and are good value. Elsewhere, there is not a great deal of choice, although there are some very pleasant small hotels in the interior, and several very acceptable ones in Arrecife. You will not find budget accommodation in the resorts. Similarly in Fuerteventura, nearly all hotel and self-catering accommodation is in the main resorts *(see Recommended Hotels, pages 126–33)*.

Hotels are rated from one-star to five-star Gran Lujo (GL). Prices within the categories may vary considerably. Prices must, by law, be displayed in hotel reception areas. Breakfast is usually included in the basic rate. Package holidays tend to be the most economical, offering accommodation in large, comfortable hotels and self-catering apartments, usually with pools. Some are known as Aparthotels. Even if you don't want to spend all your holiday in the resorts, they provide a convenient base. It is wise to book accommodation in advance, especially around Christmas, Easter and July to August.

In the interior of both islands there is a growing number of *casas rurales* – rural properties that have been converted into small hotels or renovated and rented as self-catering accommodation. For information, contact <www.turismoruralcanarias.com>.

I would like a single/ double room	**Quisiera una habitación sencilla/doble**
with/without bathroom and toilet/shower	**con/sin baño/ducha**
What's the rate per night?	**¿Cuál es el precio por noche?**
Is breakfast included?	**¿Está incluído el desayuno?**

AIRPORTS *(Aeropuerto)*

Lanzarote's Arrecife airport has two terminals. The new Terminal 1 services international flights. There is a good range of shops, car-hire desks, restaurants, exchange facilities and ATMs. Thursday is 'change over' day in Lanzarote's resorts, which means the departures section can be very busy; avoid travelling on a Thursday if you can. The airport is about 6km (4 miles) west of Arrecife. There are plenty of taxis available, plus a regular bus service to Arrecife (No. 22/23, approximately every half-hour, €0.90).

A taxi from the airport to Arrecife costs about €6, to Puerto del Carmen around €10, to Costa Teguise €12 and to Playa Blanca €28. Arrecife airport information, tel: 928 846 001.

Taxi service, tel: 928 814 655.

Fuerteventura's airport is modern and efficient. It is situated about 7km (4 miles) south of Puerto del Rosario and about 9 km (6 miles) north of Caleta de Fuste. Buses run to Puerto del Rosario and Caleta de Fuste every half-hour (€1 to Puerto del Rosario, €2 to Caleta de Fuste). A taxi from the airport to the capital costs about €8, to Caleta de Fuste about €12 (all rates valid as of 2006). Fuerteventura airport information, tel: 928 860 600.

Taxi service, tel: 928 850 059/210.

B

BICYCLE HIRE *(Bicicletas de alquiler)*

Road bikes, mountain bikes and scooters can be hired in most of the resorts *(see What to Do, page 85)*.

BUDGETING FOR YOUR TRIP

Lanzarote and Fuerteventura are relatively inexpensive compared to many European destinations. To give you an idea of what to expect, here's a list of some average prices in euros. A euro was worth approximately £0.67 and US$1.26 at the time of press.

Accommodation: Rates for two sharing a double room in high season can range from as low as €50 in a basic apartment or at a *pensión* or hostal (although there aren't many of these) to as much as €400 at a top-of-the-range five-star hotel. A pleasant three-star hotel, which is where you will find the majority of accommodation, will cost in the range of €100–€120. Rates drop considerably out of season, except at Christmas and Easter – although for some reason October is expensive in some hotels. Bear in mind that rates quoted on websites do not bear much relation to what you will have to pay. Most people go to these islands on deals that include flights and accommodation, which usually means that room rates are lower than they first appear.

Attractions: The major attractions such as the Manrique sites and Cueva de los Verdes charge around €7–8; smaller museums around €3–5. More expensive are the family attractions such as the Jardín Tropical and the Aquapark, but these are places where you can easily spend half a day, and there are reductions for children.

Bike hire: between €8 and €12 a day, depending on bike and number of days for which it is hired.

Buses: inexpensive. For example, you can go from Arrecife to Puerto del Carmen or Costa Teguise for €1.

Car hire: Including comprehensive insurance and tax, rates are around €25–40 a day from the big international companies; you get a better deal if you book for a week and if you book in advance. There are many competing firms in the resorts that will offer lower rates; cars booked in advance via the internet may also be considerably cheaper (see CAR HIRE).

Getting there: Air fares vary enormously, with those from the UK to Lanzarote ranging between £100 in November up to £400 in August (€145–€585), with spring and early-summer flights somewhere in between; budget airlines are, of ccourse, cheaper. From the US, flights cost around $900–1,000. To Fuerteventura they range between £100 in November to around £280 (€145–210) in

August – the lower summer price compared to Lanzarote due to the fact that there are *only* budget flights to Fuerteventura. The cheapest flights are usually available via the internet, and booked well in advance, or by taking a chance on a last-minute offer.

Meals and drinks: The cheap, three-course set meal called the *menú del día* is found less on these two islands than it is in most other parts of Spain. The average price of a three-course à la carte meal, including house wine, will be about €25–30 per person, but you can pay a lot less. At the top restaurants you may pay nearly twice that, but there are very few of these.

Petrol: very cheap by UK standards – around €0.80 a litre.

Taxis: Prices are controlled, and reasonable. From the airport to Puerto del Carmen the fare is around €10.

I want to change some pounds/dollars	**Quiero cambiar libras/dólares**
Do you accept travellers' cheques?	**¿Acepta usted cheques de viajero?**
Can I pay with this credit card?	**¿Puedo pagar con esta tarjeta de crédito?**

C

CAMPING

There are three official campsites on Lanzarote (all June–Sept only), but they do not offer much in the way of space or facilities:

• Camping El Salao, Isla Graciosa, tel: 928 845 985
• Camping San Juan, Famara, tel: 928 845 985
• Camping de Papagayo, Papagayo, Playa Blanca, tel: 928 173 724

On Fuerteventura there are no official campsites, but rough camping seems to be tolerated in some places; it is wise to check with the local tourist office first.

CAR HIRE (*Coches de alquiler;* see also DRIVING)

You must be over 21, sometimes 24, to hire a car, and to have held a valid driving licence for at least 12 months. You need your passport and a major credit card. It is not easy to find a vehicle with automatic transmission. There are dozens of local companies in the resorts, and these tend to be cheaper, but do check that the cars are reliable and make sure you know what insurance you're getting: comprehensive with full damage waiver (*todo riesgo*) is more expensive but can save you money, as a mere scrape in a car park can otherwise cost you quite a lot. It may also be cheaper to hire a car via the internet before you leave home. Cabrera Medina is the biggest and most respected of the local companies, with numerous outlets in the resorts and in Arrecife as well as at the airports. The big international companies (Avis, Europcar, Hertz) also have offices at both islands' airports and in the resorts.

- Avis <www.avis.com>
- Cabrera Medina <www.cabreramedina.com>
- Europcar <www.europcar.com>
- Hertz <www.hertz.com>

I'd like to rent a car for one day/week	**Quisiera alquilar un coche por un día/una semana**
Please include full insurance.	**Haga el favor de incluir el seguro a todo riesgo.**

CLIMATE

The islands have some 300 days of sunshine a year and an average annual temperature of 20°C (68°F), with midsummer temperatures soaring to 30°C (86°F). There is little rain – what there is mostly falls between October and January. The average sea temperature around the islands is 23°C (72–73°F) in high summer (July–September), and around 18°C (64°F) in winter.

CLOTHING

Light summer clothes, sandals and a swimsuit are all you need for much of the time, but bring a sweater or jacket for cooler evenings and windy boat rides, and strong shoes if you want to do any walking. A jacket for men and a smart dress for women is appreciated, although not obligatory, in the more expensive restaurants. Don't offend local sensibilities by wearing swimwear or very skimpy clothing in city streets, museums or churches, although you can get away with almost anything in the resorts.

CRIME AND SAFETY

Crime rates are not high, but there is some opportunistic bag-snatching and pickpocketing in tourist areas, especially in crowded places such as markets or at fiestas. Robberies from cars are probably the most prevalent, so never leave anything of value in a car. If you have one, use the safe deposit box in your room for valuables, including your passport (carrying a photocopy of your passport is a good idea). Burglaries of holiday apartments do occur, too, so keep doors and windows locked when you are out. You must report all thefts to the local police within 24 hours for your own insurance purposes.

I want to report a theft.	**Quiero denunciar un robo.**

CUSTOMS AND ENTRY REQUIREMENTS *(Aduana)*

Most visitors, including citizens of all EU countries, the US, Canada, Ireland, Australia and New Zealand, need only a valid passport to enter Gran Canaria. No inoculations are required. Although the islands are part of the EU, there is a restriction on duty-free goods that can be brought back to the UK. The allowance is 200 cigarettes or 50 cigars or 250g tobacco; 1 litre spirits over 22 percent or 2 litres under 22 percent, and 2 litres of wine.

D

DRIVING

Driving conditions: The main roads are generally well surfaced and well signposted – although signage in the north of Lanzarote can be a bit arbitrary. There are lots of roundabouts, but no traffic lights outside Arrecife. The rules are the same as in continental Europe: drive on the right, pass on the left, yield right of way to vehicles coming from your left on roundabouts, but give way to vehicles coming from the right at junctions. Use your horn when approaching any sharp bends. In rural areas, be aware that you may come across a very slow tractor or a large pothole. In Fuerteventura goats may also stray into your path.

Speed limits are as follows: 100km/h (62mph) on dual carriageways/motorways, 90km/h (52mph) on primary roads, 50km/h (30mph) in built-up areas and 40km/h (25mph) in residential areas, all unless otherwise posted.

There are only a couple of stretches of motorway, around each of the capital cities and their airports, and they are toll-free.

Traffic and parking: In Arrecife traffic can be heavy, parking difficult and the one-way system confusing. Early afternoon (island lunchtime) is a good time to get in and out of town, and you are more likely to find a parking space. In Puerto del Rosario parking is rarely a problem. Elsewhere on the islands there are very few traffic jams or parking problems.

It is an offence to park facing the traffic. Don't park on white or yellow lines. Blue lines indicate pay-and-display parking areas.

Petrol: Petrol is much cheaper than in the UK and the rest of Europe. Unleaded petrol is *sin plomo*. A few of the larger petrol stations are open 24 hours, and most accept credit cards. In the interior of the north of Lanzarote and the interior of Fuerteventura there are fewer petrol stations (*gasolineras*), so don't run too low on fuel.

Rules and regulations: Always carry your driving licence with you. Seat belts are compulsory. Children under ten must travel in the rear. Don't use a mobile phone while driving. Obviously, don't drink and drive.

Road signs: Apart from the standard pictographs you may encounter some of the wordings listed below.

Traffic police: Armed Civil Guards (Guardia Civil) patrol the roads on motorcycles. In towns the municipal police handle traffic control. If you are fined for a traffic offence, you may have to pay on the spot or take your fine to the local town hall.

aparcamiento	parking
desviación	detour
obras	roadworks
peatones	pedestrians
peligro	danger
salida de camiones	truck exit
senso único	one way
Useful expressions:	
¿Se puede aparcar aquí?	Can I park here?
Llénelo, por favor.	Fill the tank please.
Ha habido un accidente.	There has been an accident.

E

ELECTRICITY *(Corriente eléctrica)*

220 volts is standard, with continental-style, two-pin sockets. Adaptors are available in UK shops and at airports. American 110V appliances will need a transformer.

EMBASSIES AND CONSULATES *(Embajadas y consulados)*

If you lose your passport, or run into trouble with the authorities or the police, contact your consulate for advice.

Ireland: Calle León y Castillo 195, Las Palmas, tel: 928 297 728.
South Africa: Honorary Consulate, Calle Mendizábal s/n, Las Palmas, tel: 928 333 394.
UK: Calle Luis Morote 6, Las Palmas, tel: 928 262 508.
US: Calle Martínez Escobar 3, Las Palmas, tel: 928 271 259.

Where is the American/British consulate?	**¿Dónde está el consulado americano/británico?**

EMERGENCIES (*Urgencias;* see also EMBASSIES, HEALTH, POLICE)

Here are a few important telephone numbers, which are common to all the islands:

General emergencies:	112
National police:	091
Local police:	092
Guardia Civil:	062
Traffic police:	928 315 575
Ambulance:	061
Fire brigade:	080

Police!	**¡Policía!**
Help!	**¡Socorro!**
Fire!	**¡Fuego!**
Stop!	**¡Deténgase!**

G

GAY AND LESBIAN TRAVELLERS

Friends of Dorothy Holidays, tel: 0870 609 9699, <www.friendsof dot.com>, cater to the interests of gay travellers of both sexes; for more information, visit <www.gayinspain.com/canarias>.

GETTING THERE

By air: There are numerous budget airline flights from most UK airports to **Lanzarote**, and British Airways has scheduled flights from Gatwick and Manchester. British Airways, tel: 0845 773 3377, <www.britishairways.com>. The flight time is about four hours. Iberia flies from London Heathrow but via Madrid, which makes it a long journey, <www.iberiaairlines.co.uk>.

There are not so many direct flight options to **Fuerteventura**, but Thomas Cook has a number of direct flights, <www.flythomas cook.com>; flights operated by a number of other airlines can be found through <www.flydeals.co.uk>.

Check the web and advertisements in the travel sections of Sunday papers for good flight-only deals. Many people go to the Canaries on all-in package holidays, which can be the cheapest way to do it.

At present there are no direct flights from the US, but several transatlantic carriers, such as American Airlines, Iberia and Air Europa, have flights via Madrid, although sometimes you also have to make a connection in Las Palmas; the overall flight time is about 12 hours. Connections can also be made via London airports; check with a travel agency, or visit <www.opodo.com>.

Inter-island flights are operated by Binter Airlines, tel: 902 391 392 or 928 579 433, <www.bintercanarias.es>, for information, or book through any travel agency. The flight from Las Palmas de Gran Canaria to Arrecife takes about 45 minutes.

By ship: The Trasmediterránea ferry company runs a weekly service from Cádiz to Las Palmas de Gran Canaria and from there there are regular services to Puerto del Rosario and Arrecife. For details, tel: 902 454 645 or check the website <www.trasmediterranea. es>. Naviera Armas (tel: 902 456 500 or 928 517 912 in Playa Blanca, <www.naviera-armas.com>) has services three times a week from Gran Canaria to Fuerteventura and to Lanzarote. Naviera Armas runs ferries from Playa Blanca, Lanzarote, to Corralejo, Fuerteventura, seven times daily; crossings take about 35 minutes. The Fred Olsen Shipping Line, tel: 902 100 107 or 928 495 040, <www. fredolsen.es>, runs the *Bocayna Express* catamaran from Playa Blanca, Lanzarote, to Corralejo, Fuerteventura, seven times a day; the journey time is about 20 minutes (both lines have only five sailings on Sunday). Although they are more expensive, the advantage of the Fred Olsen sailings, for anyone who is not staying in the south of the island, is that there is a free bus service from Arrecife and Puerto del Carmen, which also calls at the airport.

There is also a new service, run by Naviera Armas, from Puerto del Rosario to Tarfaya in Morocco, journey time about three hours. At the time of writing timetables and prices have not been released.

H

HEALTH AND MEDICAL CARE

Non-EU visitors should always have private medical insurance, and athough there are reciprocal arrangements between EU countries, it is advisable for UK citizens and other member nations to do the same, because the arrangements do not cover all eventualities. The European Health Insurance Card (EHIC) entitles UK citizens to reciprocal medical care. You can apply for one online (<www.ehic.org.uk>), by phone (tel: 0845 606 2030) or by picking up a form at a main post office. Only treatment provided under a state scheme is covered, so before being treated make sure the doctor or service is working within the Spanish Health Service. Leave a photocopy of the card with the hospital or doctor. Dental treatment is not available under this system. Hotel receptionists or private clinics should be able to recommend dentists.

Hospitals: The main hospital in Arrecife is Hospital Insular, Avda Olaf Palme (Puerto de Naos), tel: 920 000 000.

In Puerto del Rosario: Hospital General, Ctra General del Aeropuerto Km 1, tel: 928 862 000 or 920 531 799.

Red Cross (Cruz Roja), tel: 928 812 222.

Private clinics: In the resorts on both islands there are private clinics where you will have to pay for treatment on the spot and reclaim it on your medical insurance. Most have English-speaking staff.

Private clinics in Lanzarote:
Branches of Clínica Lanzarote offer 24-hour service, including home visits and dentistry services. They are located at:
• Costa Teguise: Avda Islas Canarias, tel: 900 100 450.
• Puerto del Carmen: Avda de las Playas 5, tel: 928 513 171.
• Playa Blanca: Hotel Lanzarote Park, Calle Limones, tel: 928 517 643.
    The Deutsch Britische Klinik medical centres are highly visible in all the resorts, and are reliable.
    Hospiten Lanzarote, <www.hospiten.com>, in Calle Lomo Gordo, Puerto del Carmen, provides 24-hour emergency assistance, freephone: 900 707 777, otherwise tel: 928 596 100.

Private clinics in Fuerteventura:
• Corralejo: Centro Médico Brisamar, Calle Nuestra Señora del Carmen, tel: 928 536 402.
• Caleta de Fuste: Salus, Centro Comercial el Castillo, Local 15, tel: 928 163 445.
• Costa Calma: Costa Calma Medical Centre, tel: 928 875 300.
• Morro Jable: Centro Médico Morro Jable, Edificio Don Carlos, Local A, Playa Matorral, tel: 928 540 333.

Farmacias: Most problems visitors experience are due to too much sun, too much alcohol or food that they are unused to. These problems can often be dealt with by *farmacias* (chemists/drugstores). Spanish pharmacists are highly trained and can often dispense medicines over the counter that would need a prescription in the UK. They are open during normal shopping hours; after hours, at least one in each town remains open all night. Called the *farmacia de guardia*, its location is posted in the window of all other *farmacias* and in the local papers.

Where's the nearest (all-night) chemist?	**¿Dónde está la farmacia (de guardia) más cercana?**
I need a doctor/ dentist	**Necesito un médico/ dentista**
sunburn/ sunstroke	**quemadura del sol/ una insolación**
a fever	**fiebre**
an upset stomach	**molestias de estómago**

HOLIDAYS *(Días festivos)*

1 January	*Año Nuevo*	New Year's Day
6 January	*Día de los Reyes*	Epiphany
1 May	*Día del Trabajo*	Labour Day
30 May	*Día de las Islas Canarias*	Canary Islands' Day
16 July	*Nuestra Señora del Carmen*	Our Lady of Carmen
25 July	*Santiago Apóstol*	St James' Day
15 August	*Asunción*	Assumption Day
12 October	*Día de la Hispanidad*	National Day
1 November	*Todos los Santos*	All Saints' Day
6 December	*Día de la Constitución*	Constitution Day
8 December	*Inmaculada Concepción*	Immaculate Conception
25 December	*Navidad*	Christmas Day

Movable dates:

Carnaval	In February or March. Later than on Tenerife and Gran Canaria so the dates do not clash; different towns celebrate on different dates for the same reason.
Jueves Santo	Maundy Thursday
Viernes Santo	Good Friday
Corpus Christi	Corpus Christi (mid-June)

L

LANGUAGE *(Idioma, lenguaje)*

The Spanish spoken in the Canary Islands is slightly different from that of the mainland. For instance, islanders don't lisp when they pronounce the letters c or z. A number of Latin American words and expressions are used. The most common are *guagua* (pronounced *wah-wah*), meaning bus, and *papa* (potato). In tourist areas basic English, German and some French is spoken, or at least understood.

The *Berlitz Spanish Phrasebook & Dictionary* covers most of the situations you may encounter during your travels in Spain and the Canary Islands.

Do you speak English?	**¿Habla usted inglés?**
I don't speak Spanish.	**No hablo español.**

M

MAPS *(Planos)*

Most tourist offices will give you free maps, which should be sufficient. If you want something more detailed, you can find road maps in most gift/souvenir shops and supermarkets for around €2.50.

Do you have a map of the city/island?	**¿Tiene un plano de la ciudad/isla?**

MEDIA

Radio and television *(radio; televisión)*: Many hotels have satellite TV with several stations in various languages, including CNN. TV

Canarias is a local station which includes some English-language news and tourist information in its programming. English-language radio stations include Radio FM 95.3 Mhz, Power FM 91.2 Mhz and Waves FM 96.8 Mhz.

Newspapers and magazines *(periódicos; revistas)*: Major British and German tabloids are on sale in the resorts on the day of publication, but English broadsheet newspapers are a bit more scarce. British and German magazines are widely available. The English-language Island Connections (fortnightly), <www.newscanarias.net>, has island news and tourist information.

For anyone who speaks Spanish, the island newspapers are *Canarias7* and *La Provincia*. Both of these contain listings of events so they can be useful, even if your Spanish is very sketchy, but they do concentrate more on Gran Canaria and Tenerife.

Have you any English-language newspapers?	**¿Tienen periódicos en inglés?**

MONEY *(Dinero)*

Currency: The monetary unit in the Canary Islands, as throughout Spain, is the euro, abbreviated €. Banknotes are available in denominations of €500, 200, 100, 50, 20, 10 and 5. The euro is subdivided into 100 cents, and there are coins available for €1 and €2 and for 50, 20, 10, 5, 2 and 1 cent.

Currency exchange: Banks are the preferred place to exchange currency, but *casas de cambio* also change money, as do some travel agencies, and these stay open outside banking hours. The larger hotels may also change guests' money, but the rate is slightly less advantageous. Both banks and exchange offices pay less for cash than for travellers' cheques. Always take your passport when changing money.

Credit cards: Major international cards are widely recognised, although smaller businesses tend to prefer cash. Visa/Eurocard/MasterCard are most generally accepted. Credit and debit cards, with a PIN number, are also useful for obtaining euros from ATMs, which are to be found in all towns and resorts. They offer the most convenient way of obtaining cash, and will usually give you the best exchange rate, sometimes indicating the current rate on the screen.

Travellers' cheques: Hotels, shops, restaurants and travel agencies all cash travellers' cheques, and so do banks, where you will probably get a better rate (you will need your passport). It is safest to cash small amounts at a time, thereby keeping some of your holiday funds in cheques, in the hotel safe.

Banking hours are usually Monday to Friday 9am–2pm; large ones may also open on Saturday.

Where's the nearest bank/ currency exchange office?	**¿Dónde está el banco más cercano/la casa de cambio más cercana?**
I want to change some dollars/pounds	**Quiero cambiar dólares/ libres esterlina**
Do you accept travellers' cheques?	**¿Acepta usted cheques de viajero?**
Can I pay with this credit card?	**¿Puedo pagar con esta tarjeta de crédito?**

O

OPENING TIMES (*Horario comercial*)

Shops and offices are usually open Monday to Saturday, 9am–1 or 1.30pm, 4–8pm (although some close on Saturday afternoon). Large supermarkets may stay open all day and until 10pm, as do many shops in the tourist resorts, and some also open on Sunday. Banks usually open Monday to Friday 9am–2pm; post offices Monday to Saturday 9am–2pm.

P

POLICE *(Policía)*

There are three police forces in Gran Canaria, as in the rest of Spain. The green-uniformed Guardia Civil (Civil Guard) is the main force. Each town also has its own Policía Municipal (municipal police), whose uniform can vary but is mostly blue and grey. The third force, the Cuerpo Nacional de Policía, is a national anti-crime unit that sports a light brown uniform. All police officers are armed. Spanish police are strict but courteous to foreign visitors.

National police:	091 or 928 812 350
Local police:	092 or 928 811 317
Guardia Civil:	062

Where's the nearest police station?	**¿Dónde está la comisaría más cercana?**

POST OFFICES *(Correos)*

Post offices usually open Monday to Saturday 8.30am–2pm; some open in the afternoon 4–7pm, but it is better not to count on it. They are for mail, not telephone calls. The main post office in Arrecife is at Avda de la Marina 8. In Costa Teguise, it's in the Centro Comercial Maretas on Avda Islas Canarias, almost opposite the police station. In Puerto del Carmen, Avda Juan Carlos I s/n; in Playa Blanco, Avda El Correlillo s/n. In Fuerteventura, Puerto del Rosario's post office is at Avda Primero de Mayo 58; in Morro Jable, Calle Bue-

Where is the (nearest) post office?	**¿Dónde está la oficina de correos (más cercana)?**
A stamp for this letter/ postcard, please	**Por favor, un sello para esta carta/tarjeta**

navista s/n. Stamps *(sellos)* are also sold at any tobacconist *(estanco)* and by most shops selling postcards, including supermarkets in the resorts. Mailboxes are painted yellow. If one of the slots is marked *extranjero*, it is for letters abroad.

PUBLIC TRANSPORT *(Transporte público)*

There is no train service. The bus services are cheap and reliable but really only useful for getting from the island's capital cities to the main resorts; buses to other towns are infrequent. (For inter-island ferries and flights, see GETTING THERE.)

R

RELIGION *(Religión)*

The majority religion is Roman Catholic. Respect people's privacy when visiting churches.

T

TAXES *(Impuestos)*

The Impuesto Generalisado Indirecto Canario (IGIC) is levied on all bills at a rate of 5 percent. The tax is not usually included in the price you are quoted for hotel rooms.

TAXIS

The letters SP *(servicio público)* on the front and rear bumpers of a car indicate that it is a taxi. It may also have a green light in the front windscreen or a green sign indicating '*libre*' when it is free. There is no shortage of taxis in urban areas and resorts. Fares are metered, but for longer, out-of-town journeys you may feel happier

| How much is it to the centre of town? | **¿Cuánto es al centro?** |

if you agree an approximate fare in advance. Taxis are exceptionally good value: the fare from the airport to Arrecife is about €6, to Puerto del Carmen €10, to Costa Teguise about €12 and to Playa Blanca €28. On Fuerteventura, the fare from the airport to Puerto del Rosario is about €8, to Caleta de Fuste around €12.

TELEPHONE *(Teléfono)*

Phone booths *(kioskos)* accept coins and cards *(tarjetas telefónicas)*, available from tobacconists, hotels and machines that you will see in all the shopping centres – they come in denominations of €5 and €10. Instructions in English and area/country codes are displayed clearly in phone booths. International calls are expensive, so have a plentiful supply of coins or use a card. *Cabinas* or *locutorios* – cabins where you make a call and then pay at a desk afterwards – are a more convenient way of making long-distance calls.

Calling directly from your hotel room is expensive, as it is anywhere in the world.

For international calls, wait for the dial tone, then dial 00, wait for a second tone and dial the country code, area code (minus any initial zero) and the number. International Operator: 025.

Country codes: Australia 61, Ireland 353, New Zealand 64, UK 44, US and Canada 1.

Telephone codes for the Canary Islands (which must always be dialled as part of the number, even for local calls): Gran Canaria, Lanzarote and Fuerteventura 928; Tenerife, El Hierro, La Gomera and La Palma 922.

TIME ZONES

The time in the Canaries is the same as in the UK, Greenwich Mean Time, but one hour behind the rest of Europe, including Spain, and five hours ahead of New York. Like the rest of Europe, the islands adopt summer time (putting the clocks forward by an hour) from the end of March through to the end of September.

TIPPING *(Propinas)*

A service charge is sometimes included in restaurant bills (look for the words *servicio incluído*). If it is not included, then add around 10 percent, which is also the usual tip for taxi drivers and hairdressers. In bars, customers usually leave a few coins, rounding up the bill. A hotel porter will appreciate €1 for carrying heavy bags to your room; tip hotel maids acording to your length of stay.

TOILETS *(Servicios, aseos)*

Toilets in the Canaries are usually called *servicios* or *baños*. Public conveniences are rare. The proprietors of some bars and restaurants do not mind if you drop in to use their facilities, but others keep the key behind the bar to make sure their toilets are not used by the general public or, if they are, that users pay a small sum.

TOURIST INFORMATION OFFICES *(Oficinas de información turística)*

Tourist offices abroad:

• Australia: International House, Suite 44, 104 Bathurst Street, PO Box A-675, 2000 Sydney NSW, tel: 02-264 7966.

• Canada: 2 Bloor Street West, Suite 3402, Toronto, Ontario M4W 3E2, tel: 1416-961 3131, email: toronto@tourspain.es.

• UK: Spanish National Tourist Office, 79 New Cavendish Street, London W1W 6XB (mail only), tel: 020 7486 8077, fax: 020 7486 8034, brochure line, tel: 08459 400 180, <www.tourspain.co.uk>.

• US: 666 Fifth Avenue, New York, NY 10103, tel: 212 265 8822, fax: 212 265 8864, email: oetny@tourspain.es.

Tourist offices on the islands:

Tourist offices are often only open from about 9.30am–1.30pm.

Lanzarote:

• Arrecife airport: tel: 928 846 073 or 928 820 704.

• Arrecife: Kiosko de la Música, Parque Municipal, Avda de la Marina, tel: 928 811 860 or 928 801 517.

• Puerto del Carmen: Avda de las Playas s/n (next to the Fundación Manrique shop), tel: 928 515 337.
Fuerteventura:
• Airport: tel: 928 860 604.
• Puerto del Rosario: Avda de la Constitución, tel: 928 530 844.
• Corralejo: Plaza Grande, tel: 928 866 235.
• Caleta de Fuste: Avda Juan Ramón Soto Morales 10, Centro Comercial Castillo, tel: 928 163 286.
• Morro Jable: Centro Comercial, Playa de Jandía, Local 88, tel: 928 540 776.

TRAVELLERS WITH DISABILITIES

Arrecife and Fuerteventura international airports and most modern hotels have wheelchair access and facilities for travellers with disabilities, but, generally speaking, facilities elsewhere are not good. Holiday Care is a UK-based organisation that provides information, tel: 01293 774535, <www.holidaycare.org.uk>.

W

WATER *(Agua)*

The islands suffer from water shortage, so try not to waste it. Don't drink tap water. Inexpensive bottled water is available everywhere. *Con gas* is sparkling, *sin gas* is still. If you are self-catering it's cheaper and easier to buy 5-litre bottles from supermarkets.

WEBSITES

• <www.lanzarote-virtual.com> excellent site for island information.
• <www.fuerteventura.com> helpful site for general information.
• <www.tourspain.es/canarias> Spanish Tourist Office site.
• <www.spain-lanzarote.com> good all-round site.
• <www.ecoturismocanarias.com> natural parks and rural tourism.
• <www.turismoruralcanarias.com> rural tourism.

Recommended Hotels

Most accommodation on both islands is concentrated in the resorts. Elsewhere, there is not a great deal of choice, although there are some delightful *casas rurales* (rural hotels) in the island interiors, and several very acceptable ones in Arrecife. You will find very little budget accommodation in the resorts. Self-catering apartments are good value and represent a large number of the beds available. Most are in holiday complexes, some called Aparthotels, and usually offer hotel facilities such as a pool, restaurant, etc. You can also rent an apartment on a bed-and-breakfast or half-board basis.

Prices are for two sharing a double room, or a one-bedroomed apartment, in high season. Breakfast is usually included in the rates. Tax (IGIC) is extra if you book independently, but included if you book as part of a package. Prices should be taken as approximate only, and bear in mind that if you take a package deal you will usually pay less than these rates.

€€€€	over €200
€€€	€120–200
€€	€60–120
€	below €60

LANZAROTE: ARRECIFE

Arrecife Gran Hotel €€–€€€ *Parque Islas Canarias, tel: 928 800 000, fax: 928 805 906, <www.arrecifehoteles.com>*. This 17-storey hotel, recently completely renovated, is smart and glossy, with a conference room, shops, a hairdressing salon, underground parking and stunning views from the restaurant/bar on the top floor.

Lancelot €€ *Calle Mancomunidad 9, tel: 902 505 350/928 805 099, fax: 928 805 039*. A pleasant modern hotel right by the beach, with babysitting services, a pool and a restaurant with sea views. A convenient base for a short stay.

Miramar €€, *Avda Coll 2, tel: 928 810 438, fax: 928 801 533, <www.hmiramar.com>*. A plain, functional-looking building but newly renovated and right in the centre, opposite the Puente de las Bolas. Rooms are comfortable, many have sea views, and there's a bar on the rooftop terrace.

NORTHERN LANZAROTE

HARÍA

Casa Villa Lola y Juan €€ *Calle Fajardo 16, Haría, tel/fax: 928 835 256, mobile: 630 44 66 21, <www.villalolayjuan.com>*. In the heart of Haría, in the greenest part of Lanzarote. This agreeable little hotel is surrounded by fruit trees and vines. It has four double rooms and two apartments, each with a large terrace. There's a pool and a solarium.

Finca La Corona €€–€€€ *Calle La Rosita, Yé (Haría), tel: 902 363 318, fax: 928 804 209*. Set beween Monte la Corona and the Mirador del Río. There are six apartments in the main house and a converted stable block, all comfortably furnished in rustic style, with white walls and tiled floors. There's a heated pool, a children's pool, a sauna and jacuzzi and mountain bikes.

La Ermita €€ *Máguez (Haría), tel/fax: 928 842 535, mobile: 659 021 447, <www.casalaermita.com>*. Four simply furnished apartments, a communal patio and pool, in a small hotel conveniently situated for visiting the attractions in the north of the island, and about ten minutes' drive from Playa la Garrita and Arrieta.

ISLA GRACIOSA/ÓRZOLA

Apartamentos El Sombrerito € *Calle Sirena 71, Caleta del Sebo, Isla Graciosa, mobile: 696 942 874*. Seven simple apartments just a stone's throw from the harbour. Perfect peace.

Apartamentos Los Vientos € *Calle de la Quemadita, Órzola, mobile: 616 654 596*. Apartments in a pretty, traditional-style building right by the harbour.

Girasole € *Calle García Escámez 1, Caleta del Sebo, Isla Graciosa, tel: 928 842 118.* Rooms and apartments rented by the owners of this harbour-front restaurant.

CENTRAL LANZAROTE

COSTA TEGUISE

Apartamentos Celeste € *Avda de las Islas Canarias 21–25, tel: 928 591 720, fax: 928 592 482, <www.apartmentsceleste.com>.* Simple, pleasant apartments in an attractive building that is part of the Pueblo Marinero, the nicest area in the resort. Very close to the beach.

Barceló La Galea €€€ *Paseo Marítimo s/n, tel: 902 505 350, fax: 928 083 333, <www.barcelo.com>.* Comfortable, well-equipped rooms and apartments arranged around a pool in an attractive low-rise complex, built in traditional, Manrique-approved style by the beach at the west end of Playa de las Cucharas.

Gran Meliá Salinas €€€€ *Avda de las Islas Canarias s/n, tel: 928 590 040, fax: 928 590 390, <www.solmelia.com>.* Right on the beach, this hotel has luxurious rooms, faultless service, and a wonderful lobby and atrium created by Manrique, with pools, tropical foliage and statuary. Hibiscus flowers are scattered everywhere, even in the marble-walled toilets. Such pleasures do not come cheap.

Lanzarote Gardens €€–€€€ *Avda de las Islas Canarias 13, tel: 922 434 348, fax: 922 434 510, <www.h10.es>.* One- and two-bedroomed fully serviced apartments in attractive gardens grouped around two swimming pools, just back from Playa de las Cucharas. All rooms have balconies. Restaurant, poolside bar. Children's entertainment every evening, and a small playground and children's pool area. Efficient, multilingual staff. Also offers full-board packages.

MOZAGA/SAN BARTOLOMÉ

Caserio de Mozaga €€ *Mozaga, tel: 928 520 060.* An 18th-century farmhouse with a flower-filled courtyard and eight double rooms with tiled floors, wood-beamed ceilings and traditional furniture. Tradition is complemented with modernity: air-conditioning and internet access in the rooms. Great breakfasts and an excellent restaurant, open to the public *(see page 137).*

Finca de la Florida €€ *El Islote 90, San Bartolomé, tel: 928 521 124, fax: 928 520 311, <www.hotelfincadelaflorida.com>.* In the wine-producing area of La Geria, about 2km (1 mile) from the Monumento del Campesino, this attractive blue-and-white hotel offers 15 comfortably furnished double rooms and one suite. Gym, sauna, pool, jacuzzi, and tennis and mountain bikes are available.

PUERTO DEL CARMEN

Balcón del Mar € *Calle Reina Sofía 23, tel: 928 513 725, fax: 928 511 117, <www.balcondelmar.com>.* These pleasant apartments and bungalows are up a hill from the beach and harbour. It's a bit of a hike, but they are set among gardens and have splendid views and easy parking.

La Geria €€–€€€ *Calle Jupiter 5, Playa de los Pocillos, tel: 928 510 441, fax: 928 511 919.* Pleasant four-storey hotel at the quieter end of the resort. Rooms have sea views to the side, or garden/pool views. There's a landscaped pool area.

Los Cocoteros €€ *Avda de las Playas 17, tel: 928 510 361, fax: 928 510 872, <www.sunlighthoteles.com>.* Pleasant white block with Gaudí-esque chimneys. Well-equipped serviced apartments with patios. Most have sea views.

Los Fariones €€€€ *Calle Roque del Este 1, tel: 928 510 175, fax: 928 510 202.* This huge, comfortable 1960s hotel is right by the beach at the harbour end, set in lush gardens. Opposite is the even smarter Fariones Suites Hotel, under the same management.

Los Jameos Playa €€€ *Playa de los Pocillos s/n, tel: 928 511 717, fax: 928 514 219, <www.los-jameos-playa.es>.* Large hotel with

Canarian-style balconies in the spacious reception area. Rooms built around a series of white-painted courtyards.

San Antonio €€€ *Avda de las Playas 84, tel: 928 514 200, fax: 928 513 080, <www.hotelsanantonio.com>*. At the point between Playa Grande and Playa de los Pocillos, where the road becomes quieter and more residential. Looks rather clinical from outside, but is extremely comfortable and well run. Most rooms have sea views.

SOUTHERN LANZAROTE

PLAYA BLANCA

Casa del Embajador €€€ *Calle La Tegala 30, tel: 928 519 191, fax: 928 519 1922*. Unusual in Playa Blanca, this is a family-run hotel in an old house that once belonged to a diplomat (hence the name). Right by the beach, it has just 12 rooms and one suite, all well furnished and decorated. There's lots of atmosphere and wonderful views across to Fuerteventura.

Gran Meliá Volcán €€€€ *Urbanización Castillo de Águila s/n, tel: 928 519 185/928 519 132, central reservations tel: 972 894 1182*. Spacious and luxurious, this new hotel, which overlooks the Marina Rubicón yacht harbour, has 255 rooms, all with terrraces or balconies, located in 20 separate buildings. There are three conference rooms, five restaurants, several bars, four pools, a gym and spa. Caters to businesspeople and holidaymakers.

Lanzarote Princess €€€ *Calle Maciot s/n, tel: 928 517 108, fax: 928 517 011*. Part of the reliable H10 chain, this hotel is set back a couple of hundred metres from Playa Dorada beach. The air-conditioned rooms all have terraces or balconies. There are three restaurants, two pools, tennis court, volleyball, children's facilities and entertainment.

Princess Yaiza €€€€ *Avda Papagayo s/n, tel: 928 519 222, fax: 928 519 179*. Right on the beach, this smart hotel has a strong Hispano-

Arabic theme to the architecture. Five restaurants offer Japanese, Italian and Mexican food, among other styles. There's a spa, gym, pools, squash, tennis, and Kikoland, a children's playground.

Timanfaya Palace €€–€€€ *Urbanización Montaña Roja s/n, tel: 928 517 676 fax: 928 517 035*. Another in the H10 chain, this hotel on Playa Flamingo has Arabic-style architecture, comfortable rooms, a pool, billiards and snooker, a gym and all-weather tennis court, plus babysitting services and a children's play area.

UGA/YAIZA

Casa El Morro €€ *Uga, tel: 928 522 618*. Perched on a hillside, this attractive hotel offers modern conveniences and comfort in a traditional 18th-century building. Five apartments ranged round a courtyard; small pool and views over the volcanic hills.

Casona de Yaiza €€€ *Calle El Rincón s/n, Yaiza, tel: 928 836 262, fax: 928 836 263, <www.casonadeyaiza.com>*. Eight attractively furnished rooms, heated pool and jacuzzi, good restaurant in the old wine cellar, gardens full of palms and cacti. The underground cisterns – *aljibes* – have become a small art gallery.

Finca de las Salinas €€€ (**€€€€** at Christmas/New Year) *Yaiza, tel: 928 830 325, fax: 928 830 329, <www.fincasalinas.com>*. A pink-washed country house, set in attractive gardens, on the road as you drive into Yaiza from the airport. There are 19 rooms, in buildings that used to be stables, decorated in earth shades and furnished with antiques. Pool, jacuzzi and sauna, views over Timanfaya Park.

FUERTEVENTURA: PUERTO DEL ROSARIO

Hotel Fuerteventura Playa Blanca €€€ *Playa Blanca, tel: 928 851 150, fax: 928 851 158*. This former parador stands alone, right on the beach between the capital and the airport. In a distinctive – if not beautiful – building, it offers excellent service and ocean views.

Puerto Rosario JM Palace €€ *Avda Marítima 9, tel: 928 859 464, <www.jmhoteles.com>.* Opposite the port, this modern hotel has comfortable, air-conditioned rooms and friendly, obliging staff.

NORTHERN FUERTEVENTURA

CORRALEJO

Corralejo Beach Aparthotel € *Calle Nuestra Señora del Carmen 3, tel: 928 866 315.* Pleasant, functional apartments in the main shopping street, close to the beach.

Hotel Corralejo € *Calle Delfín s/n, tel: 928 535 246.* Budget accommodation close to the beach, popular with windsurfers.

Riu Palace Tres Islas €€€ *Avda Grandes Playas, tel: 928 535 700, fax: 928 535 858, <www.riu.com>.* Huge hotel on the edge of the dunes, 5km (3 miles) from the town centre, with all the facilities and comforts you would expect, indoors and out. Piano bar and children's daytime entertainment.

EL COTILLO

Apartamentos La Gaviota € *Calle Fuerteventura, tel: 928 538 567.* This large white building sits in a garden close by the harbour, flies a pirate flag and offers basic but comfortable accommodation.

Hotel Rural Mahoh €–€€ *Sitio Juan Bello s/n, Villaverde, La Oliva, tel: 928 868 050.* Early 19th-century house built of volcanic stone, with gardens, pool and multi-purpose sports pitch. Bedrooms furnished in traditional style. Environmentally-aware owners.

CENTRAL FUERTEVENTURA

CALETA DE FUSTE

Barceló Club El Castillo €€ *Avda El Castillo, central reservations tel: 902 101 001 (from UK: 0845 090 3071), <www.barcelo.com>.*

This beachside complex resembles a well-designed village: pretty bungalows set in gardens; pools, children's playground and several restaurants. Self-catering, B&B, half-board or all-inclusive.

Casa Isaítas €€ *Calle Guize 7, Pájara, tel: 928 161 402, fax: 928 161 482, <www.casaisaitas.com>*. A delightful place, white-walled with Canarian balconies and a pretty courtyard.

Casa Los Rugama €–€€ *Ctra Puerto del Rosario–Antigua Km 10, Casillas del Angel, tel: 928 538 224, fax: 928 538 081, <www. hotelrugama.com>*. An attractive country house with lush gardens and a small pool. Seven of the 13 rooms are in the main house, the others in the converted outbuildings.

Castillo San Jorge €€ *Calle Franch y Roca s/n, tel: 928 163 500, fax: 928 163 501, <www.hoteleselba.com>*. About 500m from the beach, this Aparthotel offers comfortable accommodation, in a complex with pools, sauna, restaurants, bars, etc.

SOUTHERN FUERTEVENTURA

JANDÍA PLAYA

Barceló Jandía Playa €€€ *central reservations tel: 902 101 001 (from UK: 0845 090 3071), <www.barcelo.com>*. Large hotel complex a few minutes from Morro Jable. All modern comforts in an attractive setting, plus four pools, a gym, solarium and restaurants.

Hotel Sol Elite Los Gorriones €€ *Playa la Barca, tel: 928 547 025, fax: 928 547 000 <www.solmelia.com>*. In a quiet spot at the start of the Jandía Peninsula, this large hotel offers everything you need for a relaxed and comfortable beach holiday, and is the base for the René Egli Windsurf School.

Iberostar Playa Gaviotas Hotel €€€ *Pasaje Playa 2, Jandía, tel: 928 166 197, fax: 928 166 110*. Modern hotel right on the beach; pleasant, air-conditioned rooms with terraces, a restaurant, cocktail bar, sauna, two pools and a children's pool.

Recommended Restaurants

Fish restaurants, serving fresh seafood of all kinds, line the seafronts and harbours in the resorts and coastal villages. Places serving typical Canarian food are found mainly in inland towns and villages, but there are a few in the resorts. Restaurants advertising *cocina casalinga* or *comidas caseras* serve home cooking – authentic island food. There are a few expensive venues on both islands, but most are very reasonably, and similarly, priced.

Local people eat late – lunch is at 2–3pm, dinner around 10pm – but as restaurants cater mostly to foreign visitors, they serve lunch from around midday and dinner as early as you like, and some serve food all day.

The following price guide (which is only approximate) is for a three-course meal for one with house wine.

€€€	€35–60
€€	€25–35
€	below €25

LANZAROTE: ARRECIFE

Arrecife Gran Hotel €€–€€€ *Parque Islas Canarias, tel: 928 800 000.* On the 17th floor of the island's only high-rise building. International-style food, well cooked and well presented – and the views are great.

Casa Ginory €–€€ *Calle Juan de Quesada 7, tel: 928 804 046.* In a narrow street leading from the Charco de Ginés, this small and friendly place serves good seafood and local products such as *setas* (wild mushrooms).

Castillo de San José €€–€€€ *Puerto de Naos, tel: 928 812 321.* Excellent Canarian and international food, including some imaginative puddings, served in the cool comfort of this Manrique-designed restaurant, with floor-to-ceiling windows giving views over the harbour. Smooth, efficient service – and not as expensive as you might imagine.

NORTHERN LANZAROTE

ARRIETA

El Charcón €–€€ *Calle de Nuria s/n, tel: 928 835 630*. A simple little place, right by the quay. Reliably good fish dishes.

Miguel's €€ *Calle de la Marina 37, tel: 928 835 225 or 928 848 538*. Friendly harbourside fish restaurant that also has apartments for rent. Closed in June.

HARÍA

Dos Hermanos €€ *Plaza León y Castillo, tel: 928 835 409*. In the middle of town, this busy place serves Canarian specialities such as goat *(cabra)* and rabbit *(conejo)*, as well as seafood. Always busy and bustling at Sunday lunchtime.

El Cortijo €€ *LZ10 on the southern (Teguise) exit from Haría, tel: 928 835 006*. Canarian country dishes served in an old farmhouse restaurant.

Restaurant Mirador del Valle €€ *Los Valles (LZ10 between Teguise and Haría), tel: 928 528 036*. Well-cooked local dishes are served at this *mirador* restaurant with stunning views over the surrounding countryside.

ISLA GRACIOSA

Girasole € *Calle García Escámez 1, Caleta del Sebo, tel: 928 842 118*. Close to the harbour, with a terrace and cool dining room. The garlic prawns come swimming in bubbling hot oil, straight fom the oven. You can pre-order lunch before leaving Órzola and know it will be waiting when you come off the beach.

Restaurant/Pensión Enriqueta €–€€ *Calle de la Mar Barloveto 6, Caleta del Sebo, tel: 928 842 051*. Back from the harbour, and easily recognisable by an ancient car and model ship balanced on a first-floor terrace. Reliably good fish. Also rents rooms and hires mountain bikes.

ÓRZOLA

Perla del Atlántico €€ *Avda de Caletón, tel: 928 842 525*. Set on a little rocky headland, the Perla commands the bay and serves excellent fresh fish in all the usual ways – grilled *(a la plancha)* is simple and especially good. Watch the boats to Isla Graciosa come and go while you eat.

Punta Fariones €€ *Calle de la Quemadita, tel: 928 842 558*. Harbourside restaurant; fish is the speciality, but there are meat dishes as well, mostly grilled, some with *mojo* sauces.

CENTRAL LANZAROTE

COSTA TEGUISE

El Patio €€ *Plaza del Pueblo Marinero, tel: 928 581 102*. Italian restaurant that does a good carpaccio of salmon and interesting meat dishes. Also a full range of pizzas (from a wood-fired oven) and pastas which puts it in the **€** bracket. There are wooden tables set out on a green terrace in the square.

La Graciosa €€€ *Hotel Meliá Salinas, Avda de las Islas Canarias, tel: 928 590 040*. If you want to dress up and really treat yourself, this is the place to come. Elegant surroundings, attentive service and excellent, international menu with wines to match. It's advisable, although not essential, to book. And don't even think about wearing shorts and a T-shirt.

La Ola €€ *Playa de las Cucharas, tel: 928 581 634*. Right on the beach, this open-fronted restaurant with cool blue-and-white decor has the usual offerings on the menu, but also specialises in Basque-style cooking, which means tasty and interesting. It's part of the Lani chain, which has numerous restaurants in Lanzarote, all of a good standard.

Patio Canario €€ *Pueblo Marinero, tel: 928 346 234*. One of the few places in this resort serving genuine Canarian food. There's a wide selection, including *pimientos rellenos de bacalao* (small peppers stuffed with cod, in a creamy sauce). Large, wood-panelled dining room and tables outside in a quiet, shady square.

MOZAGA/SAN BARTOLOMÉ

Caserio de Mozaga €€–€€€ *Mozaga, tel: 928 520 060*. The restaurant in this *casa rural* is known as one of the best places to eat on the island (no lunch on Mon or Tues). Excellent fresh ingredients and some wonderful puddings in the attractive setting of a converted barn.

Centro de Artesanía €€ *Monumento al Campesino, San Bartolomé, tel: 928 520 136*. Authentic Canarian food: *ropa vieja* (meat, tomatoes and chickpeas), *cabra* (goat) and *conejo* (rabbit) as well as fish, in this intriguing place. You can have tapas at the bar or at outside tables, or sit in the huge, palm-decked, domed restaurant for a full meal. Popular with local people for Sunday lunch, when nobody is in a hurry to leave.

PUERTO DEL CARMEN

El Sardinero € *Corner Calle Nuestra Señora del Carmen and Avda Varadero, tel: 928 511 933*. Cosy little fish restaurant overlooking the harbour, highly regarded by local people.

La Lonja de Fondeadero €€–€€€ *Plaza El Varadero s/n, tel: 928 511 377*. This is *the* place to eat fish. A large, two-storey dining room and a long wooden counter displaying tempting dishes. No outside tables, but it's right by the harbour, and they have their own excellent fish shop next door. Does a great *parillada de mariscos* (grilled mixed seafood).

La Ola €€–€€€ *Avda de las Playas 35, tel: 928 515 081*. Painted pale blue and white (like its cousin in Costa Teguise), with crisp tablecloths and an international menu. There is also the **Asian Restaurant** on the same site, with vivid, silky cushions and low tables, serving Thai and Indonesian food. Café La Ola has comfy white sofas and sunbeds set around a small pool by the sea, and serves good coffee and cake.

Puerto Bahía €€ *Avda del Varadero 5, tel: 928 513 793*. Another harbourside restaurant with excellent seafood and obliging staff.

Puerto Viejo €€ *Avda del Varadero s/n, tel: 928 515 265*. Excellent fish cooked by a chef known for his creativity. Frequented by local people, which is always a good sign. **El Bodegón** is a tapas bar under the same management.

TEGUISE

El Ryad €–€€ *Casa León, Calle León y Castillo 3, tel: 928 845 931*. Strong Middle Eastern influence, as the name suggests: kebabs, taboule, tajine chicken, etc. in an attractive old house with a patio. The adjoining café does coffee and cake as well as wine by the glass and plates of olives.

Ikarus € *Plaza 18 de Julio, tel: 928 845 332*. Cosy, red-walled rooms. Local fish and meat dishes and lots of varieties of pasta.

La Cantina €–€€ *Calle León y Castillo 8, tel: 928 845 109*. A series of small rooms and a patio to choose from in this old house. They specialise in *cherne* (stone bass), *corvina* (sea bass) and other local fish. Very busy at Sunday lunchtime, when everyone's in town for the market.

Patio del Vino €€ *Palacio del Marqués, Calle Herrera y Rojas 9, tel: 928 845 773*. There's a small, elegant dining room and tables in a courtyard under trailing bougainvillea. They serve typical Canarian food and specialise in local cheese, ham and Lanzarote wine. Closes at 8pm, so it's a lunch, tapas or early supper venue.

SOUTHERN LANZAROTE

EL GOLFO

El Golfo €–€€ *Avda del Golfo s/n, tel: 928 173 147*. Dining areas upstairs and down, inside and out. Good paella and other rice dishes, including *arroz negra* (black rice).

Mar Azul €–€€ *Avda del Golfo 42, tel: 928 173 132*. Pretty blue-and-white restaurant with tables set right by the sea. Specialises, naturally, in seafood, fresh from the sea and prepared with care.

PLAYA BLANCA

Brisa Marina €€ *Paseo Marítimo 10, tel: 928 517 006*. Green-shuttered seafront restaurant. Lots of fish, simply grilled with *mojo* sauces; efficient service.

El Almacén de la Sal €€ *Paseo Marítimo 12, tel: 928 517 885*. Good fresh seafood and meat dishes served in the pleasant surroundings of a converted salt warehouse by the sea.

L'Artista €€ *Calle La Tegala 18–20, tel: 928 517 578*. Just one street back from the beach, but with sea views, this attractive, green-balconied restaurant serves good Italian food, from *mare e monti* to pizzas and *tiramisú*. There's a good ambience, too.

YAIZA/TIMANFAYA

El Diablo €€ *Islote del Hilario, Parque Nacional de Timanfaya, tel: 928 840 057*. Meat is barbecued over natural heat from the volcano in a large Manrique-designed restaurant with wrap-around views.

La Era €€€ *Calle El Barranco 3, Yaiza, tel: 928 830 016*. The most famous restaurant on the island, in a farmhouse converted by Manrique and an architect friend in the 1960s. The typically Canarian food is excellent and original, using the freshest ingredients, and there's an extensive wine list. Reservations advised; no beach clothes or shorts.

FUERTEVENTURA: PUERTO DEL ROSARIO

La Marquesina €€ *Calle Pisarro 6, tel: 928 530 030*. Specialities include *pimientos rellenos* (stuffed peppers) and *sama sancochada* (sea bream in a spicy stew).

NORTHERN FUERTEVENTURA

CORRALEJO

Cofradía de Pescadores €€ *Muello Chico 5, tel: 928 867 773*. Excellent fish, as you would expect at the fishermen's co-operative. *Lubina* (bass) baked in salt may be on the menu.

Cordón Blue €€ *Paseo Atlántico, tel: 928 535 554*. Small, simple place by the harbour that serves excellent grilled meat, as well as fish and salads. Friendly, prompt service.

El Rincón de Périco €€ *Calle General Linares 40, tel: 928 535 722*. It's a few metres back from the harbour, so no sea views, but the food is good. There's a *menú casero* that includes typical dishes such as *ropa vieja* and *salpicón de pescado (see page 97)*.

La Marquesina €€ *Calle El Muelle, tel: 928 535 435*. By the fisherman's statue on the harbour, this friendly restaurant is always busy with customers enjoying the fresh fish.

EL COTILLO

El Roque de los Pescadores €€ *Calle de la Caleta, tel: 928 538 713*. Tables by the lovely harbour where you can eat plates piled high with locally caught fish – even limpets, if they take your fancy.

Marea Alta €€ *Calle 3 de Abril 1979 25, tel: 928 538 687*. Attractive place on the road to the port, serves '*cocina creativa*', including *lubina en papillote*, and a good salad with mussels. Dinner only.

CENTRAL FUERTEVENTURA

BETANCURIA/ANTIGUA/PÁJARA

Casa Los Rugama €€ *Ctra Puerto del Rosario–Antigua Km 10, Casillas del Ángel, tel: 928 538 224.* The atmospheric, stone-walled restaurant with an outside terrace in this *casa rural* is open to non-residents and has a good reputation for its Canarian and Spanish dishes.

Casa Princess Arminda €–€€ *Calle Juan de Betancort 2, Betancuria, tel: 928 878 979.* This bar and restaurant opened in 2006 in a house restored by the family who have owned it for 500 years – it's said to be one of the oldest on the island. Shady bar, dining room and pretty courtyard, serving locally produced meat dishes as well as some fish and good puddings.

Casa Santa María €€ *Plaza Santa María, Betancuria, tel: 928 878 282.* In a lovingly restored 16th-century farmhouse close to the church, you can eat roast lamb *(cordero asado)*, kid *(cabrito)* and much more besides. There's also a cafeteria, serving tapas and light meals, on the other side of the road.

Don Antonio €€€ *La Vega del Río de las Palmas (Betancuria), tel: 928 878 757.* One of the best restaurants on the island, serving original dishes made with locally sourced ingredients in a 17th-century country-house setting. Lunch Tues–Sun, dinner Fri–Sat.

El Molino de Antigua € *Ctra del Sur Km 19, Antigua, tel: 928 878 220.* The restaurant (also open Sun–Mon when the museum is closed) serves traditional island food: *rancho canario* (an elaborate stew), goat, cheese, ham and *corvina* (bass) are usually on the menu.

La Fonda €€ *Calle Nuestra Señora de la Regla, Pájara, tel: 928 161 625.* Opposite the church, La Fonda serves good island food – grilled rabbit and kid *al salmorejo* (with green peppers, in a herb and garlic marinade) and other dishes with *mojo* sauces.

CALETA DE FUSTE

El Camarote €€ *Avda El Castillo, tel: 928 859 070*. A pleasant place to watch the world go by. The menu includes a range of local and international dishes served by helpful waiters.

La Paella, Barceló Club El Castillo €€ *Avda El Castillo, tel: 928 163 756*. Has a terrace right on the seafront. Lots of excellent fish and, of course, paella.

SOUTHERN FUERTEVENTURA

LA PARED

Bahía La Pared €€ *Playa de La Pared, tel: 928 549 030*. Great place, right on the beach with panoramic views from the terrace. The food's good, too.

LAS PLAYITAS

La Rampa € *Avda Miramar s/n, tel: 928 344 004*. Good selection of fish and rice dishes in this long-established restaurant.

MORRO JABLE/COSTA CALMA

Cofradía de Pescadores €–€€ *El Muelle, tel: 928 541 909*. Fish straight from the sea, along with *papas arrugadas* and other local dishes in this busy fishermen's bar/restaurant.

Don Quixote €€ *Apartamentos Santa Úrsula, Costa Calma, tel: 928 875 158*. International dishes and local specialities, all well presented.

Restaurant La Laja €€ *Avda del Mar, Morro Jable, tel: 928 542 054*. Great fish stews, such as *sancocho canario* and other seafood in a beachside restaurant.

Saavedra €€ *Plazoleto Cirilo López 5, Morro Jable, tel: 928 541 056*. Long established, with good fish, good atmosphere and good prices.

INDEX